Praise for *What Matters Next*

"Kate O'Neill has the unique ability to take the speed out of a world that is moving fast, sometimes too fast, and allow our brains to absorb things in digestible bites. Decision-making is difficult with so many variables affecting the outcomes. *What Matters Next* is a must-read for that reason."

—Faisal Hoque,
#1 *Wall Street Journal* best-selling author of
REINVENT and founder of Shadoka

"Kate O'Neill's *What Matters Next* is a transformative guide for leaders navigating the intersection of technology and humanity. With actionable insights and a compelling vision, O'Neill equips readers to encode human-centric values into our technological future. An absolute must-read for anyone looking to stand out and make a difference in our digital world."

—Dorie Clark,
Wall Street Journal best-selling author of
The Long Game and executive education
faculty at Columbia Business School

"In the ongoing and often exhausting debates about AI and the future, Kate O'Neill is a voice you can trust. *What Matters Next* is not just a masterful playbook for better decision-making. It's a catalyst for how to show up, lead, and champion humanity–today, tomorrow, and in the years to come.

—April Rinne,
Global Futurist and Author of
Flux: 8 Superpowers for Thriving in Constant Change

"In *What Matters Next*, Kate O'Neill doesn't just provide answers—she provokes the right questions. It's a guide for leaders who understand that in the race to innovate, we must preserve our purpose and the integrity of our decisions. A timely and necessary reflection on leadership ethics in a tech-driven world."

—Dan Pontefract,
Leadership Strategist and author of *Work-Life Bloom*

"If you've ever thought that tech, especially AI, would swallow up humanity, Kate O'Neill just wrote the treatise on how leaders can avoid exactly that. *What Matters Next* will help you identify what's most important to you, to those you lead, and in the future you want to create. This is the book that will lead you to sharper decisions and, better yet, meaningful outcomes."

—Carla Johnson,
Innovation Architect, RE:Think Labs

"*What Matters Next* answers the critical question of how leaders can make tech decisions that are both ethically grounded and strategically sound in a world that's moving too fast. Kate O'Neill tackles the problem of balancing rapid technological advancement with the need to prioritize human well-being. What I appreciate most about Kate's work is her real-world approach. She's not just theorizing—she's drawing from deep experience in the tech industry and a genuine concern for the human side of innovation. Kate is focused on helping leaders navigate the "Now-Next Continuum," making decisions that are not only tech-ready but also human-ready. This kind of forward thinking, grounded in empathy and strategic foresight, is exactly what we need more of in today's fast-paced world.

—Dr. Diane Hamilton,
Author of Curiosity Unleashed

"Kate O'Neill has given us practical solutions to the fast-paced decision-making challenges that leaders face when wanting to move quickly while still making ethical decisions. With the tools in *What Matters Next*, uncertainty doesn't have to cause anxiety."

—Caleb Gardner,
Founding Partner at 18 Coffees, and
former Digital Director for BarackObama.com

"*What Matters Next* by Kate O'Neill is a game-changing book for leaders navigating our complex, fast-paced world. She presents a powerful framework that challenges us to pause, reflect, and embrace the tension of uncertainty with curiosity and courage.

Her innovative model of insight and foresight equips leaders with an invaluable tool to cultivate a mindset of inquiry, enabling them to make decisions that not only address immediate challenges but also shape a better future for all. This book is an essential read for visionary leaders who understand that true progress comes from asking the right questions and embracing the journey of discovery.

This book is nothing short of transformative—it's a beacon for those seeking to lead with purpose, empathy, and foresight in an increasingly unpredictable world. *What Matters Next* is a road map for creating meaningful change and lasting impact. For any leader committed to making a difference, this is your essential guide to navigating the complexities of tomorrow, today."

—Jeanette Bronée,
Culture Strategist and Author of *The Self-Care Mindset*

"The heartbeat of business will be decided by how well we can blend technology with our humanity. Never has this been a more pressing issue than today—as AI teeters on the brink of changing not only how we define 'work' but the very essence of 'intelligence.' One of the best bridges for this gap is Kate O'Neill. *What Matters Next* allows us to pump the brakes on the speed of change... to ask the right questions and develop the right road maps so that we have the best future possible.

—Mitch Joel,
founder ThinkersOne, author of
Six Pixels of Separation and *CTRL ALT Delete.*

"In the roller coaster of modern work, *What Matters Next* shows us how to move from hanging on for dear life to steering the course with confidence. Kate beautifully breaks down why the future of work isn't just coming—it's practically sprinting towards us—and she gives us the playbook for making tech decisions that are both human-friendly and future-proof. If you want to stop playing catch-up and start making decisions that matter, this book is your new best friend!"

—Henna Pryor,
author of *Good Awkward*

WHAT

MATTERS

NEXT

About Thinkers50

Thinkers50 is the world's most reliable resource for identifying, ranking, and sharing the leading management and business ideas of our age.

Founded in 2001, the Thinkers50 definitive ranking of management thinkers is published every two years. The Thinkers50 Distinguished Achievement Awards, which recognize the very best in management thinking and practice, have been described by the *Financial Times* as the "Oscars of management thinking."

Since 2016, the Thinkers50 Radar has been identifying emerging thinkers with the potential to make a significant contribution to management theory and practice. The Thinkers50 Booklists of Management Classics and Best New Management Books, introduced in 2022, highlight the most influential management books past and present, as selected by the Thinkers50 Community.

A LEADER'S GUIDE TO

W H A T

MAKING Human-Friendly
TECH DECISIONS

MATTERS

IN A WORLD THAT'S
MOVING TOO FAST

NEXT

KATE O'NEILL

WILEY

For general information on our other products and services or for technical support, please contact our Customer Care Department within the United States at (800) 762-2974, outside the United States at (317) 572-3993 or fax (317) 572-4002.

Wiley also publishes its books in a variety of electronic formats. Some content that appears in print may not be available in electronic formats. For more information about Wiley products, visit our web site at www.wiley.com.

Library of Congress Cataloging-in-Publication Data

Names: O'Neill, Kate (Technology expert), author.
Title: What matters next : a leader's guide to making human-friendly tech decisions in a world that's moving too fast / Kate O'Neill.
Description: Hoboken, New Jersey : Wiley, [2025] | Includes index.
Identifiers: LCCN 2024036554 (print) | LCCN 2024036555 (ebook) | ISBN 9781394296422 (hardback) | ISBN 9781394296446 (adobe pdf) | ISBN 9781394296439 (epub)
Subjects: LCSH: Business enterprises—Technological innovations. | Technological innovations—Moral and ethical aspects.
Classification: LCC HD45 .O54 2025 (print) | LCC HD45 (ebook) | DDC 658.4/03—dc23/eng/20240924
LC record available at https://lccn.loc.gov/2024036554
Subjects: LCSH: Business enterprises—Technological innovations. |
LC ebook record available at https://lccn.loc.gov/2024036555

Cover Design: Paul McCarthy

SKY10092520_120224

To all the tech humanists <3

Contents

Table of Figures

Preface

This book is about how certain kinds of decisions matter more than others. In my own life, one of the biggies was moving across the country in the mid-1990s to Silicon Valley. Picture a young woman in a Toyota Camry, windows rolled down, driving aimlessly around the Bay Area. The air is crisp and carries the scent of eucalyptus trees. Alanis Morrissette's *Jagged Little Pill* CD plays on repeat. As I navigate my way through this strange new landscape, I can't help but notice the billboards advertising high-tech services such as computer chip design conversion. I recall one to this day: "MIPS 2 RISC." It strikes me then for the first time that billboard advertisements really say a lot about what uniquely defines a place's character.

The job that had lured me west to California from Chicago was in San Jose at Toshiba America Electronic Components. Fresh from my undergraduate degree in languages and linguistics—German major, Russian and linguistics double minor, concentration in international studies—I was embarking on what seemed like a pretty unexpected journey. The career I had envisioned was in translation and interpretation. I had dreams of someday working in one of those booths at the United Nations, bridging gaps between nations through language. But when Toshiba offered me a role as a technical writer, the allure of the adventure was irresistible.

As it turned out, it was a more fitting path for tech than I could have imagined. Plus, I was a prolific writer and a self-taught technologist. At a time when websites were still a novelty, I had built the website for my university's language laboratory. This was a testament to a pattern that recurred throughout my career: curiosity coupled with initiative often paves the way for innovation. So, at Toshiba, I taught myself how to stand up a UNIX server and host the files on a remotely accessible network to assist my team in accessing the hardware documentation they needed across offices. Unbeknownst to me at the time, I had built the company's first intranet.

As I dove into the Silicon Valley ecosystem, my career unfolded in a series of start-ups led by charismatic leaders. Each start-up had identified intriguing problems in diverse fields—from manufacturing to online learning to health care and, notably, online DVD rental—and had secured enough funding to explore potential solutions. I found myself drawn to these early-stage start-ups. In this fast-paced environment, my skill set rapidly expanded: content management, business analysis, project management, product management, and beyond. One common theme emerged, though: No matter my role or responsibilities, I was consistently the person most focused on the user or the customer. I became increasingly convinced that tech cannot—and should not—be isolated from humanity nor from business.

In an unexpected twist, I found that I had indeed become a translator. Not in the traditional sense of the word, but a translator nonetheless. I was the bridge connecting business needs to the tech folks, and tech constraints to the business folks. I found myself advocating for the user while analyzing technology requirements. This unique role, which I coined as being a Tech Humanist, gradually evolved for me over the years. It taught me to merge the perspectives of business, technology, and humanity into a single, coherent focus.

Fast-forward to today, my role as the Chief Tech Humanist for my own strategic advisory firm has allowed me to consult and speak for top companies, world governments, and everything in between. It has given me the opportunity to use my interdisciplinary skills—systems thinking, strategy, forecasting, and ethics—to help these organizations navigate their path forward. I could never have imagined a job so wide-ranging, so fulfilling, and with such potential for impact.

And yes, my dream of speaking at the United Nations did come true. Only, instead of translating languages, I translated the power of technology in human terms.

I should be clear: despite what the theme of this book might suggest, I've never been one to play it safe. Caution isn't my watchword. I have a playful and spontaneous nature, which is best encapsulated by novelist Tom Robbins in one of my favorite quotes: "Humanity has advanced, when it has advanced, not because it has been sober, responsible, and cautious, but because it has been playful, rebellious, and immature." But after nearly three decades in tech, I've seen the field shift toward relentless acceleration, often at the expense of people's well-being. Conversely, I've also seen how businesses outside of Silicon Valley are often *too* cautious and suspicious of tech, missing their chance to innovate and adapt. I've had to learn the benefits of a moderate approach and advise my clients to do the same.

For almost 30 years, my job has been to translate. I've translated needs, requirements, priorities, and perspectives. I've translated from the technologists to the business leaders, from the businesses to the technologists, from corporate-speak to customer needs, and back again. I've translated from the future to the present and the present to the future. And always, throughout, I've translated the voice of the user, the customer, the human. This is the most important, most challenging work. It's when I communicate the power of the underlying tech humanist ideas to leaders for whom it is new. When they adopt this way of thinking, they not only transform their companies but also shape entire industries by their example. They do better business and redefine what better business means. It's a privilege to help leaders translate their vision in ways that align with the best futures for the most people.

INTRODUCTION

A Brighter Future Requires Better Decisions

If you sense that things are moving at a staggering speed, you're not alone, and it's not your imagination. That acceleration is measurable in at least a few ways, such as computing power. You may be familiar with Moore's law, which states that every two years, you can assume a doubling of transistors on a microchip—in other words, double the computing power. From 1965 to 2015, computing power grew by a factor of 12 orders of magnitude, or indeed a doubling approximately every 1.3 years.[i]

That's exponential growth. And the thing about exponential growth is that while it's not unprecedented in nature, it's not the model of change we're adapted to. This presents us with challenges when it comes to making decisions that will make any sense just a few iterations down the road.

It's not just speed, either; it's scale, too. For years now data-driven decision-making and algorithmic optimizations set against a globally interconnected mega-network have been hurtling us forward at a dizzying speed on an incomprehensible scale. With this speed and scale comes significant consequences. Missteps can lead to unintended consequences, missed opportunities, or even lasting harm.

---

[i] Vipra, J. & Myers West, S. (2024, April 19). Computational power and AI. AI Now Institute. https://ainowinstitute.org/publication/policy/compute-and-ai

And this was before the advent of the generative AI era changed the game—or rather, upped the stakes. Since then, skills that once looked uniquely and safely human have been encroached upon. Capabilities that companies defended as their competitive advantage became tauntingly reproducible by the masses.

All of this is why I've heard often from leaders like you: amid all this chaos, decisions are getting harder to make. Why? Increasingly, we're juggling an intricate balance between the immediate needs of our current realities (**what matters now**) and our long-term hopes and future visions (**what is likely to matter**).

In the spirit of the old chestnut, "price, quality, and schedule—pick two," three factors in the tech-accelerated business environment often misalign, making wise choices feel all but impossible: future, tech, and human. You can choose the path that propels you into the **future** the farthest and fastest. While future predictions aren't always accurate, we can typically deduce among a set of options which one seems the most open to change. You'll also need to pick a winner in the **technology** you invest in. And how do any of these choices affect **human** beings over time? Are we inadvertently setting precedents that undermine privacy, that are ripe for misuse by bad actors, or by overzealous law enforcement?

We also have to be honest in confronting our own shortcomings: we don't always make the most rational decisions. The field of neuroscience has shed plenty of light on how we decide. We humans are constantly collecting information and using it to stack the decks of our perceptions and judgments. When we move to choose, we are evaluating among options to select what matches best. Classical economics, too, would have us believe we are rational beings, only ever making decisions that make sense in an objective model of value and trade-offs.

Except, as the meme goes, that's not how any of this works.

Why not? What gets in the way? Simply put: our biases.

Evolutionarily, biases have served us well. They've helped us discern patterns for survival. That animal is big; don't go near it. That unfamiliar berry is red and reminds me of the one that made me sick last time; don't eat it.

But our evolutionary heritage also favors the tendency to play it safe, even when rational assessment suggests opportunities that others might not see.

But what if we could make better, more informed decisions? What if there was a way to minimize these risks? A method to ensure that each step we take is purposeful, meaningful, and aligned with our organization's vision?

This model offers that clarity. It starts with **insights** and **foresights**. These help us leverage data, market trends, and consumer behavior, tap into empathy, understanding, and wisdom, and in so doing, they illuminate the path ahead, enabling leaders to make more informed decisions. These aren't just reactive responses to immediate problems but proactive steps toward the desired future. It's about moving forward with purpose, keeping both the present and the future in sight as we transform and innovate.

Yet here is where we take a step back and rethink what we understand by **transformation** and **innovation**.

Often, transformation is used to play catch-up, a means of adjusting to the realities of our present situation. Transformation very often is about *catching up* to "what matters now."

Innovation, on the other hand, is the kid in us who looked at a cardboard box and saw a spaceship. It's our leap into the future. Innovation is often about venturing into "what is likely to matter."

This is why it is so exciting to draw a line between these two ideas and shine a light on the *next* steps we need to move forward.

What matters next isn't disregarding the present for the future or being stuck in the now without a vision for tomorrow. It's understanding that the present and the future are a continuum. It's planting a seed today and knowing, with patient nurturing, it will grow into a tree tomorrow.

What Matters Next invites you as a reader to pause and reflect, to take a step back from your busy life and consider what truly matters to you and to those you lead and serve.

But more than just a title, it is also a question, a challenge even. What will matter most in your future? As I pondered this question while writing this book, I realized it was a question I had been asking myself throughout my career. And it's a question I've been asked, as well, by leaders like you.

I recall an interaction with a senior operations executive from a tech company who approached me in the labyrinthine halls of a tech conference after I had delivered that day's opening keynote.

She asked a question about one of the main points I'd made, and in answering I invited her feedback, at which point she looked down and got quiet. We were surrounded by exhibitors proclaiming solutions that did enough shouting: their kiosks had all the latest buzzwords—*AI, blockchain, quantum computing.* Suddenly she waved her hand wildly at it all and asked, "I guess what I'm asking is, what does any of this mean?" At first, I thought she was playing at not understanding the terminology. But as she continued, I saw where she was going: "What does all this mean for any of us? Or for our teams, for the people we serve? How can we possibly know?"

Coming up as a leader in the technology sector, I've always been fascinated with the future, always thinking about what's next. But the future is a tricky thing. It's a shifting, nebulous entity, always just out of reach. Yet we are asked to make decisions, to take actions that will have lasting impacts on this uncertain future. So how do we navigate this balance between current realities and future visions? And how do we do it so that it has any *meaning* for us, for others, for society as a whole?

I believe the answer lies in taking the next most meaningful step.

Moving toward *what matters next*, then, challenges us to break free from the perpetual cycle of problem-solving for the present. It urges us to align with what we believe the future may hold and to take a meaningful step, however small, in its direction.

Our Journey Continues

Some of what I've included in this book reflects my own journey, but it's also a conversation. It's an invitation for you to join me in this exploration of what truly matters in our fast-paced, technology-driven world. It's a call to action, to take meaningful steps toward your future, steps that are grounded in understanding and insight.

This book in a sense picks up where my last two books, *Tech Humanist* and *A Future So Bright*, leave off. It not only builds upon their foundational ideas but also explores in greater depth how to achieve those ideas. Consider this book as the next stage in the ongoing journey to the bright future that we dreamed together. This installment, though, comes with a special focus on the leaders who are at the forefront of making the crucial tech decisions that will shape our future. It examines what it takes to navigate the complex landscapes of technology and innovation, offering valuable insights and guidance to those poised to make the decisions that will take us there.

This book aims to equip you with the tools and frameworks needed to make high-quality decisions that lead to better outcomes with fewer long-term consequences.

Of course, we cannot eliminate uncertainty. Instead, we can learn to manage uncertainty, making it a navigable part of our journey rather than a roadblock. It's about taking calculated steps forward, bringing the future vision closer without losing touch with the present.

Prioritizing today's realities versus tomorrow's visions is a false dichotomy; they aren't opposites. They are a continuum. It's not a question of either-or, but rather a blend of both. Effective leadership is both/and: Both the present and the future matter, and both require our attention. The decisions we make today should lay the foundations for the road we want to travel tomorrow.

After all, it's not just about reaching the destination. It's about the journey, about the steps we take and the courage with which we take them, and the understanding we gain along the way.

■ ■ ■

The Now-Next Continuum

Imagine a line. On one end is the past, which is familiar and known. On the other end is the future, unfamiliar and unknown. In the middle is *now*, our current reality, about which we know or can know a great deal. Our task is not to jump from one end to the other, to run headlong into the future. Instead we must take meaningful and informed steps along this line to guide our organizations toward what is *next*.

But how do we do that? How do we span the present and the future? How do we make progress without losing sight of where we've come from and where we're going?

That's where the **now-next continuum** comes in. As the primary conceptual model in this book, it's really three tools in one: It is a bridge across time, guiding us to consider our past actions and decisions in the context of present realities, as a clue to what may be knowable about the near future and predictable farther ahead. It's a tool for understanding transitions, both large and small, and for managing the complexities of our tech-driven world where change often feels too fast. And it's a map that helps us identify the most probable outcomes in the future and the most preferred outcomes and understand the effort it might take to narrow the gap between those two points.

Harms of Action vs. Inaction

The concepts in this book are powerful tools for decision-making. They guide us to act in small, incremental yet meaningful steps that don't exceed our understanding of the technology or its consequences. We know we won't reach the mountaintop in one leap, so we take one step at a time, adjusting our course as we go.

But let's be clear, this is not a green light for timid incrementalism. It's not about hiding behind caution when bravery is needed, or avoiding action when inaction could cause harm.

This difference matters when the **harms of inaction** outweigh the **harms of action**.

This paradox highlights the dual challenges of tech leadership: some companies go too fast, racing ahead of their understanding of consequences and impact, causing harm through their **actions**. Other companies lag behind, lacking the boldness they need to overcome the problems they could solve through more courageous action. In their case, harm is caused through their **inaction**.

We need leaders to have bold visions of the future, visions that harness the power and potential of tech while prioritizing equity, balance, and sustainability.

To realize these visions without racing beyond our current knowledge or understanding of potential harms and consequences, *What Matters Next* advocates for incremental action. It's about taking a small, carefully monitored step, evaluating the feedback, gaining insights, and adjusting accordingly before taking the next steps toward the future.

What if uncertainty about the future leaves you feeling stuck? Even then, this book can help. It provides a way forward, guiding you to take thoughtful and ambitious steps, as aware as we can be of potential consequences. It's about being brave, but not foolhardy; careful, but not paralyzed by fear.

Weighing the harms of action versus harms of inaction does more than just help us make decisions. It also provides a counter to the common bias toward risk aversion. It pushes us to consider the future risks that could be associated with current harms. It reminds us that inaction, too, can be a form of risk.

Commitment to Purpose

For companies to truly progress, they need to go beyond just taking the next logical step. Instead, they should be committed to a road map guided by purpose: a clear, defined sequence of steps that lead them profitably toward goals that matter more than money.

After all, success isn't just about making a profit. It's about making a difference. There's a purpose that fuels you, and it may be to drive innovation, solve complex problems, or make the world a better place. Whatever it is, this vision becomes a guiding light, illuminating a path forward.

But what does this commitment look like in practice, especially in a world that's constantly changing?

Purpose should be closely related to a company's core organizational strategy and lived every day through its operating model. Day-to-day decisions should be based not just on profits, but on values.

This is where humanistic and ethical considerations take shape. They help us consider the impact of our actions, not just on our bottom line, but on our customers, employees, and the world at large. Aligning decisions through purpose means they tie together our insights and understanding and help us avoid unintended consequences.

It's not just about taking the next *logical* step. It's about taking the next *meaningful* step, the one that takes you closer to your purpose. It's about making the kind of progress that makes you nimbler, wiser, more adaptable, and more aligned with humanity and a brighter future overall.

Freeing Ourselves for the Future

Moving toward what matters next is a bit like stepping off a treadmill and taking to the road. We stop running in place, only dealing with the present, and start taking meaningful steps toward what we believe our future holds.

This journey involves soul-searching. It requires shedding the weight of what mattered before and freeing ourselves to embrace the future.

It's easy to become entangled in blame for past mistakes, regret over what used to matter to us, and anxiety about what lies ahead. Yet, when we concentrate on moving toward what matters next, we can dream bolder dreams about what will matter in 10 or 20 years, not to act on those dreams immediately, but to ensure our next steps align with this grand vision and carry us in the right direction.

The Next Challenge

The challenge for leaders is to artfully blend our immediate needs, **what matters now**, with our hopes for the future, or **what is likely to matter**.

In short, we need you to create bold visions for not only effective technology, but equitable technology. Not just fast, but fair. Powerful, yet progressive. We need leaders who make decisions that go beyond mere profit, to consider potential pitfalls. Leaders who guide organizations that listen, adapt as needed, and then take the next meaningful step, again and again.

Ultimately, decisions that prioritize equity, fairness, and the well-being of all stakeholders are what truly matter next.

With this mindset, we advocate for a significant shift in our decision-making perspective: from technology that simply functions well to technology that works well for everyone.

Future Ready, Tech Ready, Human Ready

Most of all, this is meant to be a *guide*. It's a collection of lessons learned through practice, offered to you for your own practice.

No disrespect to academics, but this isn't meant to be a scholarly treatise on decision-making. I'm not writing as a neuroscientist who studies, say, which lobe of the brain lights up when making decisions under duress—although that would undoubtedly make for fine reading. Instead, I have spent my career in and around technology strategy in business, making influential decisions of my own, and then over the past decade, advising leaders around the world on their own significant decisions at great speed and scale. My aim here is to distill the insights I've collected from across the span of that experience and to provide you with the same truth-speaking, the same compassionate guidance I would offer to a client.

Moreover, our goal here isn't speculative futurism. We don't need to take inventory of every kind of cutting-edge technology and its potential far-reaching impact to understand the patterns. What we need is a strategic map to understand the patterns. I've never fully identified with the "futurist" label anyway. What this book reflects is my approach to futurism as a strategist.

When you're an idealist, strategy is how you get pragmatic.

And there's more than enough idealism to go around: read between the lines, and you'll see plenty of it, nestled in between all the strategic models. There's a belief that business can thrive *and* be a force for human thriving. There's a lifelong fascination with technology and its potential. There's a genuine love for the wide world of people I've met on my travels, and a wholehearted concern for their well-being.

And there's a belief in the power of transformative leadership to integrate all these priorities. So more than anything, this book is meant to help *you* transform. The discussion, diagrams, and tools I've provided are there to help you see the world and the future a little differently: to make more sense of it, to proceed with greater clarity and confidence, and to make decisions you can feel proud of.

PART I

A World That's Moving Too Fast

CHAPTER 1

The Conflicting Challenges of Leading in the Too-Fast World

In 2020, as the world was battling a pandemic, the American Civil Liberties Union (ACLU) was taking on another fight: suing Clearview AI, a then-burgeoning tech start-up, for violating privacy rights. Clearview, a facial recognition company that used AI to match faces to identities, had been collecting the faceprints of millions of people around the world, according to the ACLU suit, but there was at least one jurisdiction where that data was protected: Illinois. Collecting the facial biometric data of Illinois residents without their consent was a violation of the Illinois Biometric Information Privacy Act (BIPA). After two years, Clearview settled the lawsuit, agreeing to a nationwide ban on selling its database to most private companies and requiring opt-in consent from Illinois residents before capturing faceprints.

Why did the ACLU go to such lengths? And why should we care? Because, at its core, this case illustrates one of the most significant challenges we face in our technologically driven world: the tension between the promise of the future and the realities of the present.

Don't get me wrong. Facial recognition is an exciting technology. It boasts benefits other technologies can only dream of: convenience *and* security, identifying criminal perpetrators, locating missing persons, speeding through airport security, making unlocking a phone easier for visually impaired people or those with mobility limitations—or anyone with their hands full in the grocery line. All of it sounds incredible. But to deliver on all those wildly exciting promises, the tech asks for a big trade-off: trust and vulnerability. The sheer volume of data and the kinds of data needed, as well as the integration of that data between private and public services, *and* the lack of transparency in the algorithmic processing—all of these factors make it hard for experts to recommend that facial recognition is ready for primetime. But companies such as Clearview have raced ahead to create offerings built on datasets that one might argue (especially if you're the ACLU) compromise the security or privacy of the public. At least for now.

The Extreme Approaches to Strategic Leadership

As we solve the day-in, day-out, year-over-year challenges of leadership, particularly in the realm of technology and innovation, we draw from an array of decision-making approaches. Perhaps at times the urgent priorities of today make the thought of tomorrow's consequences feel irrelevant; perhaps at other times our ambitions for the future lead us to make ruthless sacrifices in the present. Depending on our perspectives, values, and biases, we may tend to give weight in our decisions to one side at the expense of the other. These tendencies fall somewhere along a range from favoring the present to favoring the future. At either extreme, we find two polarized tendencies: shortsightedness and longtermism. We can find many examples of both throughout the history of business and technology, and plenty of each alive and well today. Our own ability to make savvy tech decisions stands to improve by studying the shortcomings of each side, because each of these extremes can lead us astray if we don't carefully integrate our approach.

Longtermism: Overstepping the Present

On one end, we have the longtermists, who are leaders so focused on the future that they risk causing harm in the present. Their intentions are usually noble—they aim to preemptively solve future problems. But their zealous focus on tomorrow can inadvertently leave today's people to suffer. This approach can race too far ahead of our collective understanding and cause harm by amplifying existing biases and problems. That's the facial recognition scenario: a futuristic solution riddled with ethical concerns we're left to face in the present day.

In his book *What Do We Owe the Future?*, William MacAskill, a Scottish philosopher and ethicist, presents a case for longtermism. He argues that we should privilege the long view, making investments that will yield benefits for distant generations. From this angle, it might even seem rational to abandon Earth and set up shop on Mars, or to delegate all decisions to a superior synthetic intelligence.

However, this line of thinking can be too limiting, too exclusive. As Émile P. Torres insightfully writes in Salon: "When MacAskill implicitly asks 'What do we owe the future?' one must wonder whose future he's referring to. The future of indigenous peoples? The future of the world's nearly 2 billion Muslims? The future of the Global South? The future of the environment, ecosystems, and our fellow living creatures here on Earth? (Torres 2022)."

This critique is a stark reminder: we must not lose sight of the people and living creatures of today in our quest for a better future. Ahead of us is not the only direction worth caring about; around us matters too.

Shortsightedness: Sacrificing the Future

On the other end of the spectrum, we find the shortsighted. These leaders are so bound to the present that they overlook the call of the future's potential, leading to inaction that can cause exponential long-term harm. Their reluctance to commit to future-focused actions often causes them to lag behind our collective understanding, failing to control forces that could have been managed with foresight.

Climate inaction is a classic example. Despite knowing for many years how crucial it was to contain carbon emissions, too few companies and too few governments have made efforts serious enough to meet the demand. Every additional climate benchmark we don't meet causes exponentially more damage, much of which we will likely never be able to undo.

Two Flavors of Future–Ready Flaws

	Sacrificing the Future for the Present	**VS**	Sacrificing the Present for the Future
Characterized by	hesitation, lack of commitment		impatience, lack of coherence
Flaw	too shortsighted		too longtermist
Risks	Harms of Inaction		Harms of Action
Who is most harmed?	people in the future		people in the present and near-future
Errs on the side of	falling too far behind our collective understanding, what moment calls for, what market expects		racing too far ahead of understanding
How does it cause harm?	by allowing forces to scale that we didn't control while we could / when we had the chance		by the embedded biases and harms that it can allow to scale
Better approach	empathetic transformation to catch up + meaningful innovation		empathetic innovation + reconciling transformation to clean up messes behind it

Figure 1.1 The two extremes of future-ready flaws.

Integrating the Extremes

This tension between the present and the future can make it feel as if they're at war. On one side, we have our urgent priorities of today—matters that demand our immediate attention. On the other side, we have our ambitions for the future, which can seem elusive and hard to grasp. Again and again, their priorities seem to conflict. But as we know very well in our rational minds, the present and the future are not in conflict at all; they are tethered as a continuum. Which means the actions and decisions we make today—as well as those we do not make—shape the actions and decisions we will face in the future.

The challenge, therefore, is to strike a balance between these two extremes, to blend the urgency of now with the foresight of later. The rapid pace of technological acceleration and the scale at which it operates adds layers of complexity. Ethical considerations come into play, and the uncertainty of the future can be daunting. Each decision we make has consequences, and sometimes these consequences can be severe.

Yet, complexity should not deter consideration. Instead, it should spur us toward iteration and continuous improvement. This does not mean hastily launching initiatives and fixing issues on the fly. It means developing strategy, acknowledging missteps, learning, and making necessary corrections. By asking the right questions and determining the right metrics, we can transform the unknown into the foreseeable, enabling us to make future-ready decisions.

Transformation and Innovation

The key to avoiding these extremes of shortsightedness and longter-mism is an integrated approach—**transformation** and **innovation**. This isn't merely resorting to buzzwords; our approach recasts the two as part of a continuous journey to help us mediate the pressing needs of the present and the potential promises of the future.

Consider the transformation of print media to digital formats, for instance. It was a response to the present demands of readers wanting access to news anytime, anywhere. On the other hand, innovation can be seen in how Tesla propels us toward a sustainable future vision with their work on electric vehicles and renewable energy solutions. Both transformation and innovation should be guided by insights, foresights, and meaningful questions.

But planning for tomorrow while navigating today's challenges might feel a bit like driving an unfamiliar road while trying to read a map. In the rain. At night. Do you focus on the road, the direction you're headed, or that flashing alert on the dashboard? As drivers, we typically know how to juggle these tasks. Dashboard alerts indicate trouble, so they demand our immediate attention. Barring emergencies, though, we ideally use clearer moments to review our course and ensure we're heading the right way. And most of the time, our focus remains on the stretch of road right in front of us.

This can be framed as asking, "What matters now—the rain? What is likely to matter in the future—reaching our destination?" If we only thought about and reacted to the immediate concerns such as the rain without considering our eventual course, it would be too reactive and we'd never get where we mean to go; if we only ever dreamed of our destination, our immediate issues might cause us to crash before we get there.

Effective leadership focuses not just on what matters now but also on what's likely to matter. For example, an effective leader in a tech firm might address immediate software glitches (what matters now) while also investing in R&D for future product updates (what's likely to matter in the future). The best, most meaningful step forward into the future—which you determine to shape through your actions and decisions—is an exercise in integrating these viewpoints into **what matters next**.

The key is to maintain a consistent balance, though not always at the same level, between addressing immediate concerns and anticipating future needs. It's about being responsive to present circumstances, like a retailer stocking up on masks during a pandemic, while also preparing for future ones, like investing in e-commerce capabilities to cater to an increasingly digital consumer base.

In the chapters that follow, we'll explore this balance in more depth, discussing the roles of transformation and innovation with concrete examples and case studies. We'll discuss a helpful approach to developing insights, foresights, and meaningful questions that can guide us in making complex decisions.

We are confronted with a paradox: much of technology decision-making occurs amid the conflicting challenges of acceleration and hesitation. Let's explore why these extremes can lead to outcomes we want to avoid.

The Challenge of Acceleration

It's 1991 on a college campus in downtown Chicago. I'm in the dusty, dank, fluorescent-lit cavern that is the computer lab, signing into my school Internet account. This is a daily ritual, a digital check-in to see if any friends scattered across universities nationwide have sent me an email. I lower myself onto a hard molded-plastic chair in front of an all-black screen as a few sentences of administrative text scroll up from the bottom to welcome me in a nondescript light gray monospace font, while an underscore cursor prompts me to log on with my university-supplied credentials and then blinks slowly and dimly as it waits.

At this point of the early '90s, the entire Internet looks this way. Aside from my email, sometimes I log into Gopher, a file hosting and retrieval service developed at the University of Minnesota. Other times I might use FTP for uploading and downloading files, or Usenet to participate in online discussion forums. But they all look the same and feel the same: each of the services as monochrome and text heavy as the last, demanding that you know the specific syntax or commands that work in each protocol. This was the Internet at its most sophisticated.

Even Lynx, a rudimentary "browser" connected to the then-novel concept of the World Wide Web, was no different. The screen remained steadfastly black and white, the only variation being the text-based hyperlinks. The arrow keys on the keyboard became navigational tools and hitting "return" would transport me to whichever link I'd highlighted. Useful stuff, sure; sometimes handy, occasionally interesting, but those were the highlights of a largely utilitarian system.

Until one day, everything changed. A friend who worked in the university's information technology department introduced me to a new tool that had just been created by someone named Marc Andreessen at our sister school downstate in Urbana-Champaign. It was called the Mosaic browser.

This was a seismic shift in technology, a moment that people unfamiliar with the early days of the Internet—or those who weren't self-proclaimed "computer people" at the time—might not remember. But there was indeed a time before the Web as we know it today. But the Internet, as a network infrastructure, had existed for decades before the advent of the World Wide Web, the interconnected pages of content we associate with the Internet today. And that pre-Web Internet, with its miscellany of haphazard protocols and interfaces as varied as they were arcane, was a sleepy, text-heavy place.

The Mosaic browser changed it all. Formatted text, inline images? A *graphical* web browser? What was this sorcery?! It was one of the few times in my life I can recall having what can best be described as a mind-blowing experience. I can still distinctly recall the tingling sensation at the nape of my neck, the electrifying thought reverberating in my mind: "This is going to change *everything*."

The Dawn of the Acceleration Era

And change everything it certainly did. The Acceleration Era was born. The impact was monumental; it was as if we were children delightedly playing with a handful of oddly shaped pebbles, only to be handed a model spaceship LEGO kit. Suddenly, the world seemed full of endless possibilities.

Throughout the latter half of the 1990s, society began to reshape itself in the image of the web browser. Communication, music, shopping—everything started to happen online. And for this part of the origin story, the world has Marc Andreessen more than any single person to thank (or blame) for that. As the cocreator of Mosaic—that early graphical browser—and then cofounder of Netscape, Andreessen played a pivotal role in catapulting the browser from a simple tool to a star that lit the path for the web-driven economic transformation to follow.

Were it not for Andreessen's contributions and the groundbreaking work of his teammates at the University of Illinois' National Center for Supercomputing Applications, were it not for Mosaic and Netscape, there would most likely have been no Amazon, no Google, no Netflix. No Facebook, no Twitter. No FanDuel, no Pornhub. (Like I said: thank him or blame him.)

As for Marc Andreessen, he has gone on to become one of the most significant venture capitalists of the explosive tech era, cofounder of venture capital firm Andreessen Horowitz and funding numerous start-ups that have become household names today. Given his relentless pursuit of pushing the tech boundaries, it's not surprising that Andreessen is a staunch advocate of tech advancement.

His strong views on the subject became particularly evident in October 2023 when he published "The Techno-Optimist Manifesto." This document swiftly gained traction on social media, sparking a flurry of intense discussions and debates. The manifesto cited the economic theories of Milton Friedman and equated ESG, sustainability, and tech ethics with a mass demoralization campaign. It named "patron saints" and "enemies" of tech. It painted a picture of an ideology where unchecked and unregulated capitalism reigns, with seemingly little regard for the impact or consequences of its actions. It was as close as you can get to a war cry for accelerationism, a rallying call for tech enthusiasts to plow ahead at full speed. It's worth our time to explore what this means.

Acceleration as a Force

In the tech world, acceleration is often felt as a force—a driving power of rapid change propelling us faster and faster into the future. It's what makes everything feel as if it's changing all the time.

Part of this is linked to the growth in computing speed we talked about earlier, as reflected in Moore's law, which predicts that computing power will double roughly every two years.

The rise in AI-driven experiences, from voice assistants such as Alexa to recommendation algorithms on Netflix, is a double whammy: it both increases the user perception of acceleration and further ups the need for faster hardware. A 2023 publication from the AI Now Institute reported that "before the deep learning era, the amount of compute used by AI models doubled in about 21.3 months; since deep learning as a paradigm took hold around 2010, the amount of compute used by models started doubling in only 5.7 months" (Vipra 2024).

Hardware gains are only part of the story, though. The past few decades have also seen efficiencies in programming languages, evolutions in algorithms, enhancement in connectivity due to the spread of broadband and 4G (and now 5G), and increasing global cooperation and competition fueling tech advancement.

Because of those interconnected factors, the Tech Humanist impact of all this growth may be better encapsulated by Bell's law. According to this theory, every decade sees a hundredfold increase in computational capacity, and that gives rise to a completely new class of computers. Each generation of machines is notably smaller but offers the same, if not more, functionality than its predecessor.

Depending on your age and engagement with technology, you may have experienced these waves of transformation firsthand. The 1970s, the decade I was born, marked the advent of minicomputers, which began to replace the mainframes that had been prominent in the 1960s. The 1980s gave birth to personal computers, such as the iconic Apple Macintosh and IBM PC, followed by laptops such as the PowerBook and ThinkPad in the 1990s, and the transformative iPhone and Android smartphones in the 2000s.

In the decades ahead, we may see further innovations around wearable technology, such as advanced versions of Google Glass or Apple Watch, or implantable nanotechnology. While computing devices have been shrinking in size, they have also become more portable, more woven into the fabric of our day-to-day experiences.

Of course, that has also meant that every modern consumer is buying new devices more frequently to replace the old, outdated ones that no longer run the latest software. Those replacements come at a cost, and this, too, is a form of accelerationism.

Acceleration as a Cost

As we move forward at this increasingly rapid pace, there is an undeniable cost to this acceleration. It's not just a matter of dollars and cents but also of our well-being, the environment, and the overall human condition.

The impressive computing power we now take for granted doesn't come without a significant ecological price tag. For instance, the production of each new generation of smartphones requires rare earth elements such as neodymium and dysprosium, used, for example, in the magnets contained in the speaker and microphone, which are extracted via mining processes that are environmentally destructive (Mining.com 2021) and that often take place in developing countries, where labor is cheap and regulations are lax. This leads to exploitation of workers who are exposed to harsh, often hazardous working conditions (Carvalho 2017).

The environmental impact doesn't stop at extraction. As we continually upgrade our devices, we generate a mountain of electronic waste. The United States alone produces around 6.9 million tons of e-waste annually, making it the fastest-growing stream of municipal waste in the country (EPA 2021). Globally, we generate a staggering 40 million tons of e-waste each year—the equivalent of throwing away 800 laptops every second (The World Count n.d.).

This isn't just a waste disposal issue. Many electronic devices contain toxic substances such as lead and mercury. When improperly disposed of, these toxins can leach into the soil and water, causing widespread environmental damage and posing serious health risks to local communities.

As we think about the impacts of technology on the planet, we may wonder about the phenomenon of acceleration within natural systems. And in fact, the parallels between accelerated growth in technology and nature are striking. In nature, accelerated growth often correlates with shorter lifespans and reduced sustainability (Metcalfe 2003). Consider the mayfly, which lives for just a day in its adult form, or "boom and bust" algae blooms, which deplete their own resources and collapse rapidly. These examples may serve as cautionary tales for an accelerated tech-driven trajectory.

Balancing Economic Growth and Human Well-Being

At this point, you might be wondering whether I have suddenly morphed into an economist. Rest assured, I'm not claiming to be an expert in the field. However, I am interested in economic positions or the nuances of market dynamics, especially as they pertain to technology and its impact on humanity.

A phrase I often find myself repeating is: "*The economy is people.*" It's a simple statement, yet it underscores an important point. In our pursuit of revenue and profit measures, human well-being can be all too easily overlooked. Yet, it should be a prime driver in determining our overall success.

Markets, while important, are not the sole indicators of success. A more comprehensive, holistic approach to prosperity and growth is necessary. After all, if through our growth and scaling, acceleration, technological achievement, our ultimate goal is not to improve the human condition and elevate societal well-being, then what is it? And not in 10 000 years for some distant descendant of modern humans, but now, for the people living and struggling and suffering today. None of this is to suggest we abandon our pursuit of technological advancements. Rather, it's about acknowledging the cost of acceleration and making informed, ethical decisions that consider the human and environmental impacts as part of an integrative strategy.

Acceleration as a Philosophy

As in Andreessen's manifesto, accelerationism stakes out a position where unbridled and unhindered growth is the epitome of optimism. Just as the manifesto painted a picture of a future driven by unregulated capitalism and unhindered growth, adherents to this approach often envision a future in which technology reigns supreme. But little discussion is given to the impact or consequences of technology at this scale. In this world, unfettered capitalism and unhindered growth is inextricably linked to belief in the promise of a brighter, more prosperous future.

By this view, acceleration is not just a force, but a philosophy. The term favored by many of the tech elite is "effective acceleration" (often abbreviated to e/acc). It's worth a slight tangent to mention that a semi-related movement is effective altruism (often abbreviated to EA), which holds that money can empower better outcomes and has gradually come around to accepting that AI systems may be a driver of future change. But the EA folks seem to believe in some guardrails around technology. Effective accelerationists? Not so much.

The accelerationist ethos is embedded in the DNA of Silicon Valley. It was exemplified by that most Zuckerbergian mantra, "Move fast and break things."

But what if the things we break in our haste are the very things that matter most—our values, say, or civil rights? Or a sense of our human selves?

This vision of the future, while exhilarating to some, is deeply concerning to me. We want to go as fast as we can in the pursuit of progress while going no faster than our understanding of harms allows us, ethically, to go.

Move Fast, but Don't Break Humanity

The answer must lie in shifting our perspective. Yes, we want to go fast. Yes, we want to innovate. But we must also realize that our responsibility extends beyond just making a profit or being the first to market. We have a responsibility to people—our employees, our customers, and the broader society. To the planet. And yes, to the future. We need to ensure that our haste does not lead to harm.

What if we shift the "Move fast and break things" perspective to "Move fast, but don't break humanity"? How different would our decisions be?

Ethical Acceleration: The Need for Balanced Speed

It is for this reason that I call into question acceleration without ethics. We can, indeed, substitute a model of what we might call ethical acceleration. This isn't about stifling innovation or slowing progress. It's about making conscious, forward-looking decisions grounded in ethical considerations—that will serve us both today *and* in the future. It's about asking meaningful questions and using insights to guide our actions. It's about ensuring that our pursuit of progress does not outpace our understanding of potential harms.

Throughout history the hairiest question in ethics has been: *Whose* ethics? Who gets to say what the right approach is? And sure, if you remove ethics from the equation entirely, you silence the question— but unspoken, the question continues to lead to many problems. The only *just* way to answer the "whose ethics" question is: ethics as inclusive as possible. The considerations should err on the side of too broad, the ramifications almost too well thought-through. Our tendency is always going to be myopic anyway; we will make decisions that seem reasonable to *us*, based on *our* lived experiences, in the context of *our* surroundings. Challenging ourselves to broaden those perspectives—by bringing other voices into the mix as well as by asking better questions of ourselves—means we have a better chance of catching an error in judgment before it's allowed to, well, accelerate.

What if we could make decisions that propel us forward, but also carry us safely along the journey? What if we asked the right questions, used insights to guide our actions, and ensured our pursuit of progress didn't outpace our understanding of potential harms?

This is the approach we explore throughout this book.

Missteps and Oversights

In 2014 amid Apple's typical flashy debut of new features, they rolled out the Health app for iOS. You could track weight, calories, workouts, nutrition, etc. You could even track esoteric metrics such as how evenly you walk. But there was one glaring oversight, and it took the user audience watching the rollout very little time to recognize it—there was no period tracking.

Such a feature would be an obvious requirement to the approximately half of the population who menstruate. But the engineering teams at Apple and other large tech companies are often overwhelmingly populated by men. At the time, only 30% of Apple's employees were female, and just 20% held engineering roles. By 2021 they'd managed to increase that percentage somewhat: women by that time represented 34.8% of Apple's global workforce, and 24.4% of technical roles (Milanesi 2022).

But the point isn't how many women work in tech, and it's not about diversity overall—although those are important topics, and they figure into this discussion. This is about the reality that many of us increasingly find ourselves making decisions about tech products that have real-life consequences for people, who in many cases have different needs and life experiences from ours.

The Human Impact of Tech Decisions

At the very least, a misstep such as Apple's can lead to backlash, bad press, and loss of customer trust. But it goes beyond that. The absence of period tracking in a health-focused app can indirectly undermine women's health, when women already struggle with being taken seriously in medical contexts (Merone et al. 2022). If our aim is to align our work with the best outcomes for humanity, this is a step backward.

Correcting Course

But the redemptive opportunity with software is that there's always the next version. Apple released an update about a year later that included period tracking and a range of other reproductive health and related features. The update didn't erase the initial oversight or the harm potentially done, but their course correction was a step in the right direction.

It's worth noting the role that user feedback plays in shaping product development. This was clearly demonstrated in the case of

Apple's Health app, where user feedback directly led to the inclusion of period tracking. Moreover, their own reporting about the health and fitness platform refers to in-house clinicians who work closely with engineers, designers, and experts from leading research institutions to ensure health features are scientifically grounded and user-friendly (Apple 2022). Openness to feedback and input of this sort can become part of the process of learning that leads to more insightful decision-making over time.

Avoiding the Pitfalls of Longtermism

We've explored some of the perils of acceleration, and what can happen when we move too fast without considering the effects our decisions will have at scale. A tendency that can occur alongside this is when we prioritize the future *too much* at the expense of the present, and we find ourselves in a state of being overly longtermist. This may lead us to act beyond our current understanding and possibly harm people of today in favor of securing a hypothetically better future.

When we determine that we have skewed too far this way, strategic counterbalance can be struck through *empathetic innovation*—an approach that considers the human needs of the present while working toward a better overall future. We couple this with an approach to transformation of our current state in a way that cleans up the messes of the past and present rather than leaving them behind for future generations. Missteps are inevitable in any process of change or improvement, and they are an essential part of the learning process. We should embrace iteration as the path to improvement, but we must be careful not to rush the rollout of poorly thought-out solutions.

The Challenge of Scale and Connectedness

Understanding the dual forces of scale and interconnectedness is essential in tech. Why do our decisions feel so weighty? It's because, consciously or not, we recognize how even the smallest choices can be amplified by algorithms and shared across a globally interconnected populace.

Think about it—one tweet, one post, one seemingly minor choice can ripple outward, affecting not just your immediate circle but potentially millions. Perhaps this is at the heart of the fears around cancel culture—the perception that one wrong word can get you canceled and you will have to live with what feels like a global reckoning of your life and actions. The anxiety some people feel about this is real, even if the likelihood of its happening may be overblown.

But technology, by nature, has an incredibly amplifying effect. It has an uncanny ability to take any input and scale it exponentially. This means that whatever we put into it, whether good or bad, can expand to a magnitude that has significant impact. This is, fundamentally, the principle behind both the effective accelerationist and longtermist movements: an embrace of the hugely amplifying nature of technology for the sake of the future.

Making Human-Aligned Decisions at Scale

The vast web of connectivity offered by technology has profound implications. This is not just about how we conduct our lives publicly, but also about how we design experiences, build products, and grow companies. If we are to build a future that is not only tech-ready but also human-ready, we must learn how to make human-aligned decisions at scale.

We need to consider both the immediate and long-term consequences, the direct and ripple effects. It's like the sign in my childhood dentist's office that read, "You don't have to floss all of your teeth—just the ones you want to keep." We don't need to overanalyze every decision—only the ones with human consequences.

The Two Scales

When tech start-up founders talk about reaching scale, they generally mean gaining a rate of customer uptake and market acceptance that provides them with validation of their idea, recurring revenue from which to operate, and usage data to learn from and experiment with to improve their products. But when we talk about scale in the context of companies such as Apple, Amazon, Microsoft, and Alphabet, it's about tech-powered scale, a sheer enormity that recalibrates our understanding of the concept.

However, let's not forget the concept of the "human scale," which was popularized by Danish architect Jan Gehl. It holds that humans are the pivotal element in cities and urban planning. The designs of buildings, layout of roadways, and all aesthetic elements should interact with the human at the pedestrian level.

These principles of architecture serve as a compelling metaphor for the technology industry, as well as for any business designing human experiences with technology. How do you create great experiences for individual users, or personas of users, when you need to cater to millions? How do you balance tech-powered scale with human scale?

We'll explore that more in Chapter 5 when we discuss ethical acceleration and designing human experience at scale.

The Power of Connectedness

One of the recurring themes in my work is interconnectivity. While the idea that everything is connected might be unsettling for some, I find it reassuring and cosmically enlightening. We are connected to all the matter in the universe through the big bang. We are all made of elements forged in the explosions of enormous prehistoric stars. We are all descendants of the same single-celled organisms, and we are all part of the same species of human. And in the digital age, we are connected through networks of shared knowledge and experiences.

Social media demonstrates the power of our social graph—that is, the interconnectedness of whom we know and whom they know. When you look at a site such as LinkedIn, for example, you often find that you are only one or two degrees, or connections, away from someone famous, or a decision-maker at a top company, or even me. (Go ahead and send me a connection request!)

The work we do sets a precedent for how we want to be in the world. Scale and connectedness amplify our impact. So, even when the world seems too fast and even when our work seems too small, bear in mind: you're not just making decisions; you're shaping the future.

Avoiding the Pitfalls of Shortsightedness

Every leader has experienced a moment where the metaphorical water level starts to rise inside of their organization's boat. Panic sets in. Immediate problems demand attention, and the instinct to bail out the water—address the immediate issues—can be overwhelming. But, as any seafarer will tell you, if you don't find the source of that leak, you'll be bailing out water indefinitely, or worse: you'll sink.

That is very much what shortsighted decision-making looks and feels like. Perhaps the trade-offs and consequences don't always seem quite so clear, but they often have equally dramatic outcomes.

The Consequences of Shortsightedness

In business and particularly around technology, shortsightedness often manifests as a focus on transformation at the expense of innovation. Transformation is about adapting to the present, responding to changes that have already happened. It's the equivalent of bailing out the water. Innovation, on the other hand, is forward-looking. It's about anticipating and preparing for an otherwise unknown future. It's a bit like fixing the leak.

A successful organization needs both.

Transformation is necessary, but focusing solely on catching up can make us lose sight of the future. It's a form of "shortsighted transformation"—prioritizing the immediate at the cost of the future. And this is where the problem lies. Shortsightedness is often accompanied by hesitation and a lack of commitment. Even when we begin the work of transforming, we do so only haltingly, or we don't follow through.

The ramifications of this shortsighted approach can be catastrophic. In our haste to address immediate concerns, we may overlook emerging trends, fail to anticipate future challenges, and ignore the need for long-term strategic planning. By doing so, we risk becoming reactive rather than proactive, constantly trying to keep up with developments rather than leading the way.

A shortsighted approach, one that overemphasizes transformation at the expense of innovation, can cause exponential harm. We risk falling behind our collective understanding, the moment's call, and market expectations.

When we lose track of our organization's long-term goals, we risk falling behind in a world that's constantly evolving and accelerating.

So how do we avoid this pitfall? How do we ensure that our decisions today will not only solve the problems at hand but also pave the way for a successful, sustainable future?

Insight and Foresight

The answer lies in the power of insight and foresight. With everything changing so fast, your best chance at making good decisions is to have some of them premade. That's where having meaningful insights and foresights comes in clutch.

Insight refers to a deep understanding of the current state of affairs. It's about understanding the present in a dimensional way, knowing where we stand today. Foresight, on the other hand, allows us to anticipate future trends and develop our strategies accordingly over time. We may not know where things are heading, per se, but foresights help us keep track of the signals we pick up that offer us clues. They help prepare us for the changes yet to come.

The more we practice an insight- and foresight-driven approach, the more we have the benefits of our past wisdom already guiding us in the future.

Asking Meaningful Questions

To leverage the power of insight and foresight, we need to ask the right questions. These are not the kind of questions with easy, googleable answers. These are deeper, more complex questions that challenge us to think critically and creatively about our organization and its place in the world, about the impact of our decisions in *both* the short term *and* the long term.

We need to ask questions such as: What is our purpose? What are our values? How do our decisions affect our stakeholders? And most importantly, how can we make decisions today that will not only benefit us now but also pave the way for a sustainable, successful future?

Shortsightedness is a trap anyone can fall into. But by seeing it for the risk it is and consciously striving to correct it with insight and foresight, we can make decisions that not only solve the problems at hand but also pave the way for a successful future.

The Challenge of Hesitation

Hesitation is a sneaky beast. It can creep into our minds and hearts subtly, almost imperceptibly, making itself at home before we even realize it's there. It can be a silent saboteur, undermining our confidence and casting shadows of doubt over the decisions we've almost, nearly, just about made.

In my experience, hesitation often stems from a place of overwhelming complexity. And complexity is ever present in the world of technology—a space packed with endless potential and fraught with challenges. We're confronted with an ever-evolving landscape of innovations, shifting consumer needs, regulatory upkeep, ethical dilemmas, and the pressing urgency to adapt and grow. At times, the sheer enormity of it all can leave us paralyzed, hesitating just at the edge of action.

Even when you have invested in exploratory committees, held offsite brainstorming sessions, run the due diligence, modeled the numbers, and so on, it's all too easy to retreat into the comfort of the status quo. Perhaps we're not wholly convinced our model is defunct. Perhaps we're held by the nostalgia of tried-and-true past strategies. Perhaps the call for change is easy to resist because we don't like the alternatives.

As relatable as those hesitations are, we cannot afford to be stymied by them. We must recognize the inherent danger in complacency. There are instances where the harms of inaction can far outweigh the harms of action.

Take the tobacco and oil industries, for example. Despite mounting evidence of health and planetary harms and growing consumer demand for better-aligned offerings, there has been a hesitance to relinquish profitable business models. After all, there are clearly still cigarette smokers and clearly still gas-powered vehicles. The existing approach seems to survive and adapt, even if it is on borrowed time.

But what are the consequences of this sort of hesitation? What future are we forging through our evasion of necessary change?

The invisible-hand philosophy of the market may assume that buyers are rational and will always make the "right" choice. But history shows us that visionary leadership is often what drives significant change. Consider Tesla, a company that has pushed the boundaries of what's possible and challenged the status quo. Despite divided opinions on Elon Musk's leadership style, there is broad consensus that Tesla's commitment to battery innovation has been a game changer for the growth in sophistication of the electric vehicle market.

Such examples should inspire us to confront hesitation boldly. The dangers of inaction are real and expensive, but the rewards for audacious, progressive action can be transformative.

Our decisions today along the now-next continuum will shape the world of tomorrow. We must be cognizant of the potential unforeseen consequences of our actions and ensure our decisions align with our insights and understanding. Often, our hesitation is rational—it's a hint that our understanding needs to catch up.

Our collective unease about AI, for instance, stems from genuine concerns about societal readiness and the world's preparedness for AI systems to take a leading role in shaping decisions and experiences. These anxieties encompass everything from the ethics of data usage and deepfakes to job displacement and power imbalances. (We'll look more closely at all this in "AI's Promise and Peril along the Now-Next Continuum.")

Overcoming hesitation is a little easier with a healthy dose of curiosity and the drive to champion innovation. When we suspect our model is causing harm, we can use active empathy as a tool to help clarify our priorities. It may not always be an easy journey, but it's a vital one. Amid this dynamic, ever-evolving landscape, our role is not just to survive, but to lead our companies and communities to flourish.

Oddly enough, the world of comedy offers us an interesting parallel to leadership. The best laughs come when someone *commits to the bit*. Whether it's improv, sketch comedy, or just goofing around, a half-hearted delivery will kill the impact. A full-throated commitment will just plain *kill*. (In comedy, "killing" is good.) It could be a ridiculous scenario, but to make the most of it, you commit to the bit.

In business and leadership, the same principle applies. It's not always the decisions we make that define us, but rather the ones we hesitate on or fail to commit to. And in business, as with comedy, commitment—or lack thereof—can make or break the outcome.

Half-Hearted Commitments

Business history is littered with stories of half-hearted commitments that led to missed opportunities. Companies that saw the future but didn't fully embrace it. Take Kodak, for instance. They didn't *miss* the digital camera opportunity; they *invented* it. But despite having the foresight to anticipate the digital revolution, they lacked the commitment to embrace it fully, choosing instead to cling to their film-based business model. This lack of commitment was a primary factor in their downfall.

Or consider Blockbuster in its heyday, then the giant of video rentals. They had the chance to buy Netflix when it was a fledgling DVD-by-mail service. But they failed to see the full potential, to envision a future where e-commerce (and later streaming) would reign supreme. They did make some attempts in online rentals but didn't commit in a coherent way. As a result, they were left behind as streaming services, led by Netflix, took over.

And then there's Research in Motion (RIM), the company behind BlackBerry phones. They saw the trend toward touchscreen phones but were hesitant to let go of their physical keyboard design. Despite having the resources to adapt and pivot, their lack of commitment to this new direction led to their decline.

The Rippling Consequences of Failure

Failures on this scale can have far-reaching consequences that extend beyond the individual company. Employees face layoffs, salary cuts, or even bankruptcy, leading to job losses. Customers may face disruption in services they rely on, financial losses, and disillusionment.

Sometimes, the effects of a company's failure can ripple out to society. This is particularly true when the organization plays a pivotal role in the economy or has a significant social impact. For instance, a major manufacturing company going out of business can damage the local economy, affecting other businesses and leading to job losses in related industries. If a health care provider fails, it could leave communities without essential services. In extreme cases, these kinds of failures can even contribute to economic downturns or crises. When Nokia failed to adapt to the smartphone market, its hesitation left them open for a takeover by Microsoft. Because Nokia had been such a major employer, the impact of its demise was felt even in the national economy of Finland (Steinbock 2013).

Commit to Evolving

How can we avoid tanking whole economies with our leadership? How can we ensure that we don't just observe the future, but actively participate in shaping it for the better?

Success may rely on many factors, but at least part of the answer lies in commitment—not just to a singular decision or action, but to our purpose, to the people we serve, and to the principles that guide our actions, as well as to learning, to meaningful growth, to evolving and adapting.

It's not about prioritizing the future over the present in a self-denying sort of way or pretending that present concerns aren't real. It's about understanding that the present and the future are intertwined; that the actions of our todays lead inexorably to our tomorrows. It's not enough to anticipate the future—we must have the courage to actively participate in shaping it.

If we can envision a brighter future and we want to arrive there, we have to align our immediate needs, resources, and priorities as we plan for what's next. The most significant progress often comes not necessarily from making a giant leap but from taking the next meaningful step along the now-next continuum.

The Clarifying Power of the Now-Next Continuum

As we grapple with the complexity that comes with leading rapidly changing business and technology decisions, and since we frequently need to make decisions that not only address present concerns but also strategically position us for the future, we need a model and tools to help us do all that. Let's explore the now-next continuum.

On one end, we have the present—the immediate needs and realities we must address. On the other end, we have the future—the long-term vision we are striving toward.

Navigating this continuum requires us to be both grounded in the present and aspirational about the future. We must balance immediate needs with long-term goals and understand that the two are inextricably linked. This requires us to ask insightful questions, extract meaningful information, and use it to guide our decisions.

This, in turn, requires us to shift our thinking from merely what's knowable about the present to what's foreseeable about the future. It's about transforming our knowledge and instincts into meaningful predictions that can guide our actions. We dig more into how we do that in the sections to come.

In this model, the past informs the collective set of what is known and what mattered at that time; the present is what matters now. It's also *knowable*—we have some observations, maybe some current data, but not always up-to-the-minute information and analysis. But since whatever is past has already happened and what is just behind us in the immediate present is observable, we can generally find out whatever we might wish to know about these time horizons.

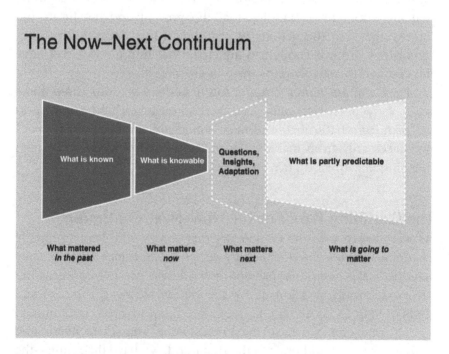

Figure 1.2 The now-next continuum.

As we look toward the future, we cannot see with certainty what *will* matter. We can foresee it to some extent, though. We can anticipate the continuing through lines of what we have prioritized up to now, such as, say, our commitment to user-friendly design; we can see patterns in the trends and current events around us, such as the increasing importance of data privacy; we can think through the trajectories of certain likely innovations and developments, such as integrating AI capabilities into our products. This gives us a sense of what is partly predictable about the future, and given that, we can begin to formulate an idea of what is *likely to matter* at that point. It may not matter yet, or it may matter but seem insurmountable. The key is to recognize that the present and the future are not separate entities but part of a continuous flow of time and experience.

Decision Tool: Questions, Insights, Foresights, Adaptive Strategy

Our challenge is to ask the right questions, gain the right insights, and adapt nimbly and strategically. Here is a list of questions to help you review what matters in your own environment and start to gain clarity on your next most meaningful actions.

What questions do you need to ask to move the knowable into the realm of the known? For example, how does our product meet the current market demands?

What understanding have you gained? Such as understanding that our customers value ease of use above all else.

What insights should guide your decisions? For instance, the insight that data privacy concerns are increasing even as consumer appetite increases for algorithmically mediated products, which have data risks. How should we operationalize this insight?

What foresights should guide your strategic direction? Perhaps the foresight that AI will play a significant part in future product development, but this must be executed with care in terms of data privacy.

Once we've assessed what we know, what we don't know, and what we could and should learn, we can create an action plan. (There is a guide to creating your action plan in the Appendix.)

Then we can begin to think about moving from the kind of transformation that will help us catch up to the kind of innovation that will move us forward. But first we need to dig a little deeper on the art of how to think about the future.

CHAPTER 2

Future Visioning

Transforming the Unknown into the Foreseeable

The future can feel abstract, but it is very much here and now. It's the moment *just* ahead of this one, and the moment ahead of *this* one. And it's concrete: it's the next *moment*, the next *day*, the next *year*. It's a very real and ever-present sense of the next moments that flow from our current states and current actions; a natural progression, not entirely a nebulous, distant time horizon; it is also the tangible, foreseeable consequences of our actions today. Of course it does include that boundless expanse: it is theoretically infinite, so it *is* that abstract, completely unknowable time horizon, as well, shrouded in uncertainty.

But the expectation isn't for you to shape outcomes a million years from now. What is expected is your ability to make informed decisions about today and tomorrow from a place of integrity; actions that align with the times we're in and which try to make sense of the times we can appreciate ahead. That's the essence of it.

And that's quite enough. To make good decisions that stand even the small-scale test of time, which you can look back on, say, a decade later with confidence, is no small feat. It means you did what you could with what you had at the time, and you looked ahead just enough. You tried to do *better* than before.

As a straightforward articulation: the future is simply the time ahead of us, and it is at least somewhat knowable and predictable because it is at least somewhat shaped and influenced by the actions and decisions we've already taken and those we are about to take today.

Vision and Agility: The Netflix Miracle

Imagine being locked in a life-or-death market struggle with your biggest opponent. Your resources are stretched thin, every dollar, every ounce of attention is focused on survival. Amid this chaos, would you dare to invest in a technology that won't bear fruit for another decade?

Netflix did. And that's the kind of vision that can redefine an industry. As one of the early employees there, I got to witness those leadership decisions up close.

In 2000, back when Blockbuster was Goliath and Netflix was David, when the very survival of the company was at stake, Netflix was already looking beyond the arena to the horizon. They were envisioning the future of entertainment, and it wasn't DVDs.

Amid the throes of this relentless quest for survival and market dominance was an extraordinary display of leadership involving two game-changing decisions. First, Netflix developed its secret weapon: the subscription model. No more à la carte rentals; now there was recurring monthly revenue. It was the beginning of a business model that would catapult the company into the pantheon of Big Tech. Secondly, they had the foresight to invest. What *did* matter at the time was beating Blockbuster and surviving in the open market. But what was *going to* matter was having the relevant technology platforms and formats in place to deliver the kind of experiences people were going to want once the company emerged alive and victorious.

So even while revolutionizing the industry, Netflix was already laying the groundwork for the next big move. CEO Reed Hastings and team had chosen to invest R&D budget into what we were then calling "set-top boxes"—the predecessor to today's streaming services. For context: this was a full six years before Roku came along and even longer before Netflix launched any kind of dedicated streaming plan.

Can you fathom the foresight required to invest in a technology that wouldn't be fully realized for almost a decade, all while locked in a fierce battle for survival? This is the kind of foresight and strategic thinking that leaders in every industry need to cultivate.

The Power of Leading with Vision in a Too-Fast World

It was the privilege of my career to get to witness that decision-making up close. And it shaped me for the years of my career since then as a leader, as a thinker, as an innovator. I learned firsthand that foresight and vision are indispensable skills, and not just in the DVD rental industry—in every industry.

In this too-fast world, organizations need to be prepared with maximum agility. They need fast-twitch muscles for "what matters now" sprints to pivot around the more whimsical forces and fads of market trends, such as competition and consumer demand. But they need the stamina and the slower-twitch muscles that can envision and endure the longer "what is likely to matter" time horizon of large-scale societal shifts.

To achieve both, you'll need good data: signal quality, clarity, data modeling that makes sense, analytical skills, reliable insights.

You'll need a culture of experimentation: agility, failure as teacher, iteration.

You'll need organizational adaptability: rigid hierarchies and bureaucracy get in the way here.

You'll need systems and scale: technologies, processes, and communications practices that add lift to the winning insights and results.

And you'll need a little something else: culture, the sense of purposeful work, alignment between the business and the people in the market, the sense that the company is in touch with the outside world.

The ability to balance immediate priorities and long-term vision was the cornerstone of the strategic leadership that boosted Netflix to success.

Uncertainty Is Everywhere

The lament I hear most often from leaders is how uncertain every-thing feels, and how daunting it is to make decisions in times that feel increasingly uncertain. With abundant data and growing algorithmic inputs, the processes that govern our work and lives feel increasingly settled—and yet, still not certain. We sense that the world we inhabit isn't in sync with where we want and need it to be. But let's take a moment to examine what uncertainty really means, why it unsettles us, and how we can reframe our focus.

The Paradox and Principle of Uncertainty

Uncertainty, a fundamental principle of physics, was first articulated by German physicist Werner Heisenberg in 1927. According to quantum mechanics, it is impossible to know both the momentum and position of a particle simultaneously. This uncertainty is inherent in the very nature of reality itself, at the smallest level of particles. This means that, at a certain level, reality is fundamentally unpredictable and unknowable.

This paradox of uncertainty might seem like a strange or even disturbing thought, but allow me to suggest: perhaps it is actually a deeply liberating one. It means that we can never really know everything, and that the universe is full of surprises.

But paradox is central to the human experience. Insights are shaped by paradoxes. We need hot to understand cold, and cold to understand hot; we need both sun and rain, light and dark. We need those things that seem to be in conflict in order to see clearly. Life is full of paradoxes, and it is through these contradictions that we gain new perspectives and greater understanding.

The uncertainty principle is just one example of a paradox that helps us to understand the nature of reality. It is a reminder that life is full of uncertainty, and that this is what makes it so beautiful and so precious. Embracing uncertainty can inspire us to live fully.

The Human Experience and Meaning Making

Philosophers have debated free will versus determinism for millennia, but one interpretation of the uncertainty principle implies that, at least at a quantum level, reality is fundamentally indeterminate. This suggests that we always have the potential to choose our own destiny, no matter what obstacles may appear in our path. (An alternative interpretation is that it is fundamentally fixed. In which case, why stress about it?)

But if we suppose that nothing has inherent meaning, and nothing is predetermined, then what does this say about the human experience? The answer is both simple and complex. On one hand, you could say it means that life is ultimately meaningless. But on the other hand, it also means that we have the freedom to create our own meaning. The choice is up to us.

Here's one way to see it: we are free to create our own meaning.

It's a paradoxical situation, but it's also a deeply human one. This quest for understanding amid uncertainty is a fundamental part of the human experience. In a world where everything is temporary and nothing is guaranteed, our focus and investment determines what gives our life meaning. There is no single answer to the question of meaning in life, but there are many possible answers.

These are potent insights as we consider what it means to scale a vision of a human-friendly future through synthetic means.

Uncertainty is, paradoxically, one of the few certain things in life. If we make peace with that, we can examine it for insights about how we may proceed, including what is *likely* to happen, and what is *likely* to matter. That leads us to probability.

From Uncertainty to Probability

When we consider a given question, such as "How well will our new product sell?" we weigh various possible outcomes. Of course we are not going to be absolutely certain, but within that uncertainty we can articulate a range of scenarios. There's a chance the product will become our best seller! There's a chance, we suppose, that it will not sell at all. But among these scenarios, some are more likely to happen than others: perhaps the product will sell in approximately the same numbers as our last products, give or take whatever factors we might know to consider, such as an expanded sales team or a multi-channel marketing campaign. In other words, even without detailed analysis, we often have a reasonable range of understanding of what could happen, what probably won't happen, and what is *likely to* happen. This is the lens of probability.

Call it forecasting, call it speculation, or call it futurism: they all take shape from different data and models. But whether you are using reported data, such as historical sales, or your instincts, honed through experience, the process you go through to make more confident decisions is progressively moving away from uncertainty toward greater probability.

As you ask what outcomes are possible and which are probable, you also have, no doubt, a preferred outcome. The strategic work becomes clearer: What effort do you need to make to make the preferred outcome more likely? Maybe sales like your last launch are most probable, but certainly you would *prefer* to have a record-setting year. It does no good to simply wish for it or even to demand it without backing it up with strategy; what specifically could you do to close the gap between the probable and the preferred outcome? This is often an exercise that can immediately shed light on practical solutions,

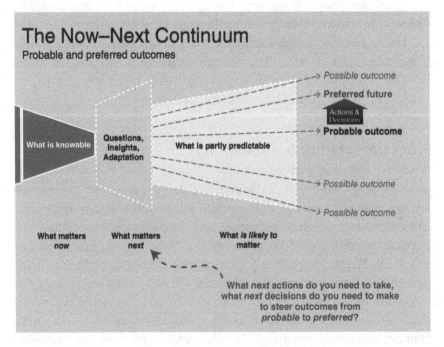

Figure 2.1 The now-next continuum and outcomes.

whether that means clarifying priorities, reallocating resources, or even hiring people dedicated to focusing on this issue.

The Practicality of Probability

Probability and improbability are familiar to physicists and mathematicians, but not always to decision-makers in other fields. Whereas certainty is a luxury we can rarely attain, probability is a skill we can continually cultivate. Embracing probability over the need for certainty makes us more adaptable, a trait needed when working with AI systems or technology, or really, in any field.

What we find is that we don't need to *know* what's coming; we just need to learn to prepare for a range of the most probable outcomes, as well as those outcomes that would be most damaging if they caught us unprepared.

That set is usually small, sometimes even binary. In other words, say you are preparing for a board meeting, and you don't know how a particular part of your presentation is going to go over. For each discussion point, you could think of it as two options: they like it, or they don't like it. Sure, it is likely to be more nuanced than that, but even that limited probability forecast tells you to prepare for both scenarios on each point, and if you do, you'll be that much better prepared for every other variable in between.

Of course, let's not sleep on improbability. What is improbable is almost always more interesting than what is probable. We'll explore why in the discussions on AI and meaning.

Tackling Uncertainty as a Team

Navigating from uncertainty to probability and toward future readiness requires not only the skills we're exploring here, but also supporting resources, such as reliable data and analysis. We need regular updates about future trends and trajectories; these can help prepare for what lies ahead. Advisors who provide honest insights and analysts who can report deeply and well are invaluable. Above all we need to cultivate teams of empowered future-ready thinkers who take these tools into their own areas of expertise and aren't afraid to voice their concerns upward and around them.

Questions for Future Visioning

We want to understand how we think about the future in as richly detailed a way as we can: the most probable outcome and your most desired outcome—and the effort needed to steer your desired outcome to become the most probable outcome. Well-formed questions allow us to do this.

Each forecasted outcome, whether it's the most probable or your most desired, can be interrogated with meaningful questions. They are the key to future visioning processes.

For example, in the context of a tech start-up, the probable future might be moderate growth, while the desired future is rapid expansion and market domination. The questions then revolve around what strategies or innovations can be introduced to shift the probable to the desired.

There's a correlation between the questions you ask and the outcomes you can envision. If you can't envision the future the way you need to, you probably have to ask better, more precise and meaningful questions.

Let's break that down further.

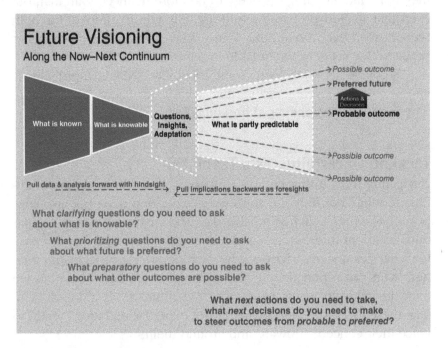

Figure 2.2 Future visioning.

Clarifying Questions

First, clarifying questions are about understanding what is currently knowable and help us understand the most probable outcome based on current realities. For instance, if you're a clothing retailer, a clarifying question could be, "What are the current fashion trends influencing consumer purchases?"

Preparatory Questions

Next, we have preparatory questions that explore what other outcomes might be possible. These questions enable us to look at different scenarios and examine how our decisions today might affect those. For example, "How would implementing a new technology influence our production process and costs?"

Prioritizing Questions

Lastly, prioritizing questions helps us decide what future we prefer. They guide us on how to steer outcomes from the most probable to the one we desire. A prioritizing question might be: "What steps do we need to take to become the leading brand in our industry?"

The Calibration Question

What do you have to do to steer outcomes from the most probable to the one you prefer? This might involve, for example, investing in research and development to create a revolutionary product.

From Questions to Actions

Asking questions is part of the work of future visioning, to help us to transform uncertainty into future readiness. But the next step is to act. Closing the gap could mean educating the marketplace or engaging in behavior change, such as a shift toward more sustainable practices. That can be a costly, difficult endeavor, but it's a meaningful one. And on a purely ROI basis, if your leadership becomes associated with the efforts to do the right thing and move toward a brighter future, it's invaluable to the relationships you have with customers and the brand value you foster.

Adidas, for example, made a sourcing and materials commitment to use only recycled plastics in their products. While there is market demand for sustainable products, this decision is still quite forward-looking. It acknowledges a gap between probable and preferred outcomes. But it readies the company for a future with greater market demand for such products. It also prepares for a scenario where non-recyclable materials are heavily regulated or even banned. This Next move toward the future positions them more solidly in the space where they can be a relevant, sustainable, innovative brand.

What are your clarifying, preparatory, and prioritizing questions? What do you need to do to steer outcomes from the most probable to the most preferable? The answers may demand effort and courage, but the rewards could be extraordinary.

Future-Ready, Not "Future-Proof"

I get asked a lot to weigh in on how future-proof some project or product approach is. That term strikes me as a bit silly. If we were talking about something being child-proof, it would mean that kids can play in your living room, and they won't poke their eyes out. Fair enough.

But your living room is not future-proof, and neither is your life, nor your marketing strategy—not even your business. Because the word "future-proof" itself suggests that there's some way to shield against the future so it won't poke your eyes out. But there's no preventing the future from happening. Remember what we determined about the future: it is simply the time ahead of us, and it is at least somewhat knowable and predictable because it is at least somewhat shaped and influenced by the actions and decisions we've already taken and those we are about to take today.

So we can't be future-proof. There's no such thing. The future is coming. What we can do, though, is be more *future-ready*. Does the choice of wording make a difference? I think it does. "Future-proof" puts you into a defensive posture, frightened of the future and denying its potential. "Future-readiness" sets you up as a leader to be prepared for the strategic complexity ahead, to face the cascading decisions that flow from this one, to face the transformation process the way an athlete faces training.

What Future-Readiness Requires

Future-readiness is not about predicting what the next big thing will be, but about fostering a flexible mindset that embraces change as a constant. For instance, a tech company doesn't need to be the very first to know the next big social media trend, but they do need to have a cultural and practical willingness to adapt their marketing strategy when that trend arises.

This readiness is not about having flawless predictions of what the future will bring, but about having a clear and coherent understanding of our purpose.

The Reality of Future-Ready Leadership

Future-readiness may seem like a tall order, especially when considering the long-term projections made by futurist organizations that span hundreds, even thousands of years ahead. But your foresight most likely doesn't need to stretch that far. You don't need to predict every technological advancement of the next century or know everything about future trends or market conditions to make informed decisions today. Instead, it's about having a clear strategy and using it to take confident, purposeful actions in light of what *is* foreseeable and how it aligns with your long-term goals.

The scope of vision should be dictated by the context and the immediacy of the decisions we need to make. It's understandable that the farther out a decision is, the less clear it will be. But the sooner a decision is due, the sharper our vision of that future timeline should be.

Balancing Present and Future

Future-readiness means balancing immediate needs with long-term impact. For example, a city may need to address a current housing shortage, but a future-ready approach would consider how today's solutions will affect the city's population growth, infrastructure, and environment in the future.

You don't want to solve problems today in a way that causes more headaches tomorrow. Similarly, it's essential not to rob future generations of opportunities to satisfy fleeting desires today.

Some needs will require trade-offs against the future, but we should strive to invest in solutions that create opportunities for future generations.

Strategic Optimism

Throughout culture and literature, the future is usually depicted as a choice between two binary outcomes: dystopia or utopia. But rationally we know that model is too limiting. Otherwise, we'd be living in a dystopia or a utopia right now, and most people would agree that if anything the present feels like a bit of both.

What the dystopia-utopia model shows us is what we fear about the future as well as what we hope for. This can be instructive. We can use what we've learned from this narrative technique to understand that our best planning for the future needs to include both a plan to mitigate the worst-case scenarios we fear and a plan to strive for the best case scenarios we hope for. This was one of the core concepts of my last book, *A Future So Bright*. I call this approach strategic optimism. In a nutshell: it's our most optimistic ideas about what the future could be, coupled with a rigorously strategic approach to make it achievable. It meshes beautifully with the now-next continuum and all the other tools we're discussing in this book.

All of which means that if the future *feels* uncertain, it's not so much that the future *is* uncertain. It might just be that your *approach* to the future might not be *strategic* enough—or not *optimistic* enough. Or both.

Purposeful Future Visioning Leads to Strategic Clarity

It is true that one of the most pressing challenges business leaders face in the too-fast world is the responsibility to anticipate and not just react to change. This requires future visioning and strategic clarity. For example, a health care organization's purpose might be to improve patient outcomes in the context of an increasingly challenging insurance landscape. This purpose, not predictions about future medical advancements, should guide their strategic decisions, such as investing in patient engagement platforms or expanding payment management services.

Strategic clarity doesn't mean we have all the answers about the future. Instead, it's about making increasingly confident decisions based on extending our purpose through insights and foresights.

Tools of Future Visioning: Prediction, Forecasting, Insights, Foresights

You don't need to be a futurist to be future-ready. What does it take to avoid the unintended or unforeseen consequences of our actions? It's not necessary to have a detailed road map of what the next 100 years will look like. Predictions, in my view, are overrated. We don't need magical powers of divination. What we need is a sense of what is likely to *matter*.

Prediction and forecasting, insights and foresights—all of these play a role in strategic decision-making. The differences between them can be subtle.

For instance, compare a prediction, a forecast, an insight, and a foresight about the wearables market. A *prediction* might claim that wearables will become the dominant technology by 2030, while a *forecast* might estimate the wearables market's size by that year. An *insight* could observe growing public comfort with wearable technology and a *foresight* might identify potential opportunities for wearables to address upcoming climate challenges.

To uncover foresights and clues about future trends, we do best to follow news and developments with the keen eye of a detective looking for clues, constantly sifting and sorting them to discern patterns and implications. My expertise lies in helping clients recognize the insights and foresights that are often hiding in plain sight, a skill honed through extensive experience across various industries, companies, organizations, and cities. It's the exposure to the wide variety of examples that makes the patterns easier to spot when they emerge.

The upshot is: less focus on predicting the future; more focus on making competent, purpose-driven decisions while maintaining strategic clarity.

Understanding how to make good decisions is a lifelong skill. Some scenarios demand immediate responses, but not all do; sometimes we benefit from taking the time for deliberation to weigh potential outcomes fully so that we can see consequences. Other times we need the self-awareness to realize that just because something isn't affecting us doesn't mean it isn't affecting other people, and we need to make those decisions in a hurry too.

Legislation around climate change is like this—policymakers often hold back, hindered by fears of political fallout from advocating from policies that are initially deemed too aggressive or restrictive. But here's the paradoxical truth made clear through future visioning: in a decade or two, we'll likely view almost any action taken today as not having been rigorous enough. Recognizing that now is future visioning in action.

Don't waste time worrying about how to predict the future with a great deal of confidence. *Prepare* for it instead.

How do we prepare for the future? By fostering an adaptive mindset through insights and foresights, by embracing change as a constant, and most importantly, by understanding our strategic purpose. Understanding our strategic purpose and considering with active empathy how our actions will impact those affected by our solutions is the key to making future-ready decisions. We explore decision-making next.

PART II

Making Human–Friendly Tech Decisions

CHAPTER 3

Future-Ready Decision-Making at Scale

The Insights-Foresights Model

Jeff Bezos once said, "As a senior executive, you get paid to make a small number of high-quality decisions. If I make three good decisions a day, that's enough" (Hu 2018). That quote also testifies that leadership isn't about the quantity of decisions, but rather their quality.

Leadership in a too-fast world brings immense pressure, with decisions needing to be made in the blink of an eye. It's easy to lose sight of long-term implications in the whirlwind of immediate problems. Or, when we do move aggressively toward future visions, it's all too easy to overlook the real-world right-now problems of people who get left behind.

The scale and complexity of decisions raise the stakes as well. Amid the rapid pace of technological advancement, the uncertainty of the socioeconomic landscape, and the urgency of global challenges, decision-making becomes an exercise not just in logic and analysis, but in courage, empathy, and foresight.

How do we do that in a world that is increasingly automated, polarized, and distracted?

Despite our best efforts, we don't always make the right call. In fact, inefficient decision-making can cost a typical Fortune 500 company around $250 million in yearly wages. That's a staggering

530 000 days of managers' time annually (De Smet, Jost, and Weiss 2019). But what if we could change that?

Deciding, Fast and Slow

A friend who served as an officer on a ship in the Navy used to tell me about a drill she and her fellow officers would sometimes have to do. You'd be below deck and signaled to race upstairs for an emergency. At the top of the stairs, you had to turn right or left immediately with no hesitation. On either side there was an obstacle or a problem to be dealt with: on the right there may have been a simulation of a fire; on the left perhaps a simulation of someone pointing a gun at you. You had to deal with whatever high-stakes situation you had randomly and inadvertently chosen and now faced. There was no turning back, no second-guessing, and no time to do anything other than react as well as you could.

Sometimes making decisions in our too-fast world feels a little like that. But most of us aren't making life-or-death split-second decisions in quite so extreme a scenario.

I wonder if our quick decisions are more likely to stem from being slightly impatient and intellectually lazy when it comes to solving problems. Don't we tend to jump to immediate answers without taking the time to fully understand the situation at hand? This pattern of thinking and rapid decision-making can be beneficial in situations where the stakes are high.

But if you have the luxury of time, resources, and the opportunity to make a more intellectually rigorous decision, seize it. It's important to consider the circumstances surrounding you, to absorb whatever relevant information you have access to, and to weigh all possible outcomes.

In doing so, you are more likely to make the best decision given the circumstances, rather than going with an immediate, potentially rash choice. This approach is about leveraging your intellectual capabilities to their fullest extent when the situation allows for it, allowing for a more thorough understanding of the problem and a more effective solution.

Slow Down to Speed Up

It's a paradox: even as the world seems to rush at breakneck speed toward the future, some decisions will be better—and more efficient—if we spend more time understanding them. Consider Google's moonshot thinking, where the company spends time pondering complex issues, such as artificial intelligence and quantum computing, to make informed decisions that have long-lasting impacts.

Sometimes decisions are hasty. When Uber introduced its ride-sharing platform, it disrupted traditional taxi industries worldwide. While it offered convenience for users, it also stirred controversies due to its brash culture of bypassing existing regulations—which also overlooked the livelihoods of taxi drivers.

Other times, we delay decisions, letting them languish on our desks while we wait for some elusive nugget of information to make a go/no-go decision. Many a hot iron has gone cold while we wait for the perfect moment to strike.

The key question here is not velocity but trajectory. Are we merely moving fast, or are we moving forward?

The art of decision-making is not just reacting swiftly to data at hand. It's having the wisdom to shift gears when needed.

From Quick Fixes to Insight-Driven Strategies

As we begin a deeper examination of decision-making, let's acknowledge that *your* answers aren't in this book. Not the *precise* answers for the *specific* dilemmas you face in your *particular* organization at this *exact* moment in time—at least not *as such*. They're not in any book. Nor are they in a keynote, a workshop, or an online course.

You don't need a one-size-fits-all solution. The quick fix doesn't exist.

And that's a good thing. That means you can create purpose-fit strategies.

Steve Jobs's decision to launch the iPhone in 2007 wasn't based on a prescriptive set of guidelines. It was rooted in a deep understanding of Apple's mission, the technology landscape, and consumer desires. This decision, although a risk at the time, revolutionized the mobile industry and transformed the way we communicate and interact with technology.

Leadership *is* decision-making. The best thing your decision can be is well researched or based on strong intuition, but preferably both.

Deciding to Decide Better

The too-fast era requires new tools for effective decision-making. This level of complexity calls for a clear-headed process: a new and more disciplined way of thinking that leads to greater clarity, easier decision-making, and a stronger sense of how to translate the future into the present.

We need to be confident in our decisions. It's not about perfection or absolute certainty. Our approach must be grounded in a set of first principles we can continually enrich that guide us with greater clarity over time.

Next, we need to have the best data available to us and the best understanding of that data. Data, in this context, isn't just numbers and statistics. It's information about the landscape that helps us understand our reality, our challenges, our opportunities, and our impact. This kind of data reflects the diversity and complexity of our world and helps us make decisions that are fair, inclusive, and sustainable.

Finally, we need to ensure we're aligned with history the way we want to be. History, in this context, is more than the past. It's an awareness of our place in the continuity of time: learning from the past, being present in the now, and shaping the future.

An example of this approach is in Microsoft's shift toward a growth mindset under Satya Nadella's leadership. The decision was rooted in a deep understanding of Microsoft's context and was guided by its values and principles, emphasizing learning, curiosity, and innovation. Microsoft has been recognized for having reinvigorated its leadership in the emerging tech industry, and its success is often attributed, at least in part, to this growth mindset culture.

Guiding Future-Ready Decision-Making with the Insights-Foresights Model

Making decisions responsibly in business, especially those involving AI, requires an approach that aligns with the fundamentals of human experience. That approach must integrate the power of technology with what's best for people, in a way that is hopeful yet pragmatic about the risks we face if we steer wrong.

Enter the **insights-foresights model (see Fig. 3.1)**. I developed this tool to deal with the complexities and contradictions of the

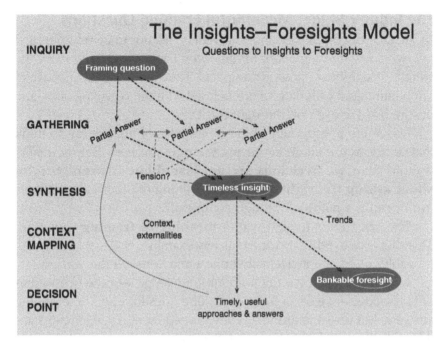

Figure 3.1 The insights-foresights model.

too-fast world. It focuses on transforming the unknown into the fore-seeable by asking progressively better questions and determining increasingly meaningful metrics. It doesn't just help us make deci-sions; it helps us foster a mindset of inquiry, cultivate insights, and harness foresight. It's about searching for the best outcomes in the face of uncertainty and standing the best chance at creating future-ready, innovative solutions.

We'll discuss each of the steps briefly below, and in greater detail in the sections that follow.

1. Start with a **meaningful framing question**.
2. Collect **partial answers**.
3. Examine the tensions between those answers to discover **timeless insights**.
4. Bring **context**, **trends**, and **externalities** into consideration.
5. Arrive at a **timely** approach.
6. Set aside **bankable foresights** to help calibrate our next actions.

The Inquiry Stage: Meaningful Framing Questions

In the face of complexity and uncertainty, it's not uncommon to feel overwhelmed and impatient for answers. These tough calls carry the weight of significant potential impacts. They are hard because we're often inundated with data, overwhelmed with the consequences, and unsure if we're even on the right track.

It's tempting, especially in these moments of uncertainty, to think that decisions are all about having the right answers. But the reality is more nuanced. **Decisions are not just about answers; they're about asking the right questions.** Shifting the focus to questions can open up a pathway through complexity.

The first step is to start with a **meaningful framing question**. This allows us to reflect on and critically examine the situation at hand. It enables us to be intellectually honest and consider the context.

In general when we think about knowledge—or the acquisition of knowledge—we often focus on asking questions and determining answers. But answers are inherently limited: contextual, circumstantial, of the moment, timely, and driven by dynamic externalities.

Rather than proceeding directly from a question to an answer, we first recognize the difference between answers and the approaches we adopt as solutions. A question may elicit many answers, but they aren't all solutions. Unlike answers, which are often fleeting and context-dependent, questions invite you back again and again. They are a renewable resource.

We also recognize a critical step in the liminal space between questions and eventual solutions: insights. It can be beneficial to dwell here, rearticulating questions to make sure we're framing the problem meaningfully, gathering partial answers, and, most importantly, allowing insights to form. Insights provide a deeper understanding and clearer path forward. We'll come back to insights in a moment.

Each time you revisit them, questions can offer more considerations, leading to deeper insights. What's more, the best thing about a great question is that it leads to an even better question. When you approach discovery this way, you have a continual cycle of exploration and understanding.

The Power of Meaningful Questions

In my early career, I was in the trenches of software development. As a young woman working around programming teams that were almost entirely made up of men—men who, it must also be noted, were often lacking in some of the more genteel social graces—I got the message fast that if I wanted questions answered, I needed to come prepared.

If I showed up at their desks with vague, open-ended questions about how the software worked, they'd slump at the shoulders, roll their eyes, make broad, patronizing statements about the purpose of the product, and wave me away to go do more research. If, however, I began our interaction by saying "I've read through the code; I get what this module is supposed to be doing. The specific question I have is what this function does because it references a variable I can't seem to get to," etc., *then and only then* did I have a decent chance of getting an informative answer. And maybe even, if the programmer got swept up in the explanation, a bonus digression about some nifty little trick the programmer had spent all last night figuring out, complete with demonstration and side lecture about what additional problems this would solve. Back at my desk, I'd still have to translate their "geek-speak" answer into "user-ese" for, say, a product manual, but I'd have gotten the information I needed to get my job done, and then some.

Over time, as I ascended into higher-level consulting roles, often with top executives at leading companies, I began to witness a nearly opposite phenomenon: *powerful leaders often ask simple questions.* The most valuable lessons in my professional growth have come from observing, during our strategic sessions, those executives who listen closely to their teams, admit when they need clarification, and ask insightful follow-up questions. It taught me with lightning-bolt clarity that uncertainty could sometimes be an asset.

What both experiences demonstrated in nearly opposite ways is that *knowing all the answers isn't nearly as valuable as knowing the right way to ask the questions.*

I Don't Know

Since then I've noticed plenty of other people who struggle, as I once did due to my professional upbringing, with the confidence to say, "I don't know." I understood the impulse in my own case: I'd always harbored plenty of curiosity and was comfortable with holding space for ambiguity and uncertainty in my own thinking, but had found it a liability to cop to professionally. For other people, I could only assume that asking questions made them feel vulnerable, and vulnerable isn't what most people like to feel in business environments.

That's what studies suggest may be at the root of the issue, anyway—and that issue is that people in business simply don't ask enough questions (Brooks and John 2024). Sure, maybe apathy and egotism are part of it for some people, but the most common reasons are likely the fear that we'll appear incompetent or unprepared. So, most of us haven't done enough practicing, and we don't have the tools to understand how beneficial effective question-asking can be.

The Anatomy of a Good Question

Good questions are the key to unlocking meaningful insights. And this is an important part of the process of determining what might matter in the distant future and what matters next. But a good question is more than just a string of words with a question mark at the end. It is a tool that can elicit in-depth responses, spark creative thinking, and foster better working relations.

We all ask questions, and perhaps we have all had the experience of recognizing a truly good question. Maybe an interviewer asked it; maybe it's something someone on our team asked; maybe we even asked it ourselves. In any case, it will help to get clearer on what exactly makes a question really *good*. While there is no single definitive answer to this question—context matters, after all—you can form better questions by looking at the traits that good questions will generally share (Ross 2009).

Good questions may be:

1. **specific**, focusing on a single issue or problem;
2. **clear**, without any room for ambiguity or confusion;
3. **relevant**, addressing a real need or problem that we are facing so that we can find a useful and actionable solution;

Or

4. **open-ended**. They may invite exploration and creativity rather than demanding a single, correct answer. This allows us to think more deeply about the problem and come up with a more original solution.

Consider for a moment the kinds of questions that help people think analytically and critically: "What are the consequences of going this route?" Exploratory questions such as "Why did this work?" can spark reflection and fresh perspectives. And a question such as "Can that be done in any other way?" can encourage breakthrough thinking.

Or consider this five-tier architecture of questioning shared in the *Harvard Business Review* article "The Art of Asking Smarter Questions": investigative, speculative, productive, interpretive, subjective (Chevallier, Dalsace, and Barsoux 2024).

Whatever approach inspires you, the most important qualifier, I have found, is to **ask questions that lead to better questions**.

The answers to our questions are often already within us. The challenge is knowing the right questions to ask. These questions need to challenge the status quo, probe deeply into our assumptions, and compel us to think about the future. They should push us to move beyond what we know to what we could predict.

Shaping the Future with Questions

In my own work, I often ponder monumental questions that pose endless opportunities for making a better future. For example, the biggest starting question in my work tends to be: *How can humanity—or rather, how can we help humanity—prepare for an increasingly data- and tech-driven future?*

This huge, open-ended question has no easy answers, but I can ask it numerous ways with different emphasis, and it always leads to many partial answers. Gathering those partial answers and thinking about what they have in common, what their relative priorities are, and so on—that's what leads to the insights and foresights that guide my work, which in turn guides how I advise my clients.

In fact, I will share a secret from my consulting playbook. In about 80% of cases when I've been able to add immediate value, it's been because I couldn't determine what question was being asked, so I've peeled back the layers of confusion by asking clarifying questions until we all have collective *aha* moments.

You can do this too. Just keep questioning your way to the root of the problem. Ask a different question. Come at it from another angle. Ask that everyone consider the same set of limitations.

As much as this process is about finding solutions, it's not *only* about finding solutions. I believe **meaningful questions are more valuable than sensible answers**. After all, the solutions we decide on today might not be *relevant* tomorrow. And one way of looking at all of this is that it's about ensuring that our solutions and approaches are relevant. Because, as you'll see in the meaningfulness model we discuss in Chapter 5, relevance is a key component of decision-making.

Tool: Mining for Meaningful Questions

Here's an exercise to help you mine for meaningful questions. Take a question you are currently considering in your business and turn it over a few different times.

- How can you make it more specific? Do you need to ask about a particular product, or a particular customer set?
- How can you create clarity? What are you currently assuming that you could spell out explicitly?
- How can you make it more open-ended? Rather than asking about what happens in Q3, reformulate the question to consider the next 10 years. What changes?

This exercise might make you uncomfortable, and some of these exercises will conflict with one another. That's okay—the goal is to stimulate insightful thinking and uncover new perspectives.

The Gathering Stage: Collecting Partial Answers

Of course, it only takes asking one question to know you're going to end up with more than one answer. We've all been there. You're in a leadership meeting, a brainstorming session, or a strategy roundtable, and you pose a question to the group. Then, you brace yourself for the flurry of answers. Only, there isn't a consensus. The marketing team is excited about the potential market share, but the engineers are concerned about the tight deadline. The sales team is worried about the product's complexity and how it will be received by customers. You're faced with a mosaic of differing perspectives—each one a piece of the overarching puzzle, but none providing the complete picture.

The Gift of Partial Answers

And yet, there is immense value in this very scenario. The ambiguity in those conflicting viewpoints holds the potential to unravel game-changing insights.

It's no secret that most of the answers you receive in such scenarios only speak to one person's experience. They're *partial answers*, fragments of the truth, each one colored by the unique perspective of the person offering it. They are not necessarily wrong answers; they're simply incomplete. They may not provide a clear solution, but they expose different facets of the situation. In fact, most answers are only partial answers, and that can sometimes leave us feeling like there are no answers at all.

But we must accept that as part of the process. We're not going to *answer* our way out of complex and difficult times. That's because every answer is generally only one consideration, and they're only good for now, in this moment, under these circumstances. And as quickly as we come up with answers, the circumstances change, and we have to go back to the questions. But as long as we keep asking better questions that prompt us to keep figuring out what matters, we can keep leading ourselves to more meaningful insights.

From Conflicting Answers to Insights

Once we have a few partial answers, perhaps that seem to contradict one another, we can begin to explore the tension between them to find some kind of timeless truth, some kind of guiding insight.

In my own experience, insights have proven to be immeasurably more valuable than partial answers. I've seen firsthand how the ability to derive insights from conflict can transform decision-making processes, helping leaders make more informed, strategic choices.

How do we find insights among multiple conflicting partial answers? One approach is to look for tension and examine it closely, like peering through a microscope at the cells that compose an organism.

The tension between answers is where the magic lies. When we adjust our lens to view these contradictory answers in context, we can begin to see the fuller picture. We can extract the golden insights that lie in the tension between these fragments of truth.

Tension signals turbulence, and that means conflicting perspectives, conflicting priorities, or change. It can be a powerful signal that something is shifting, that something new is emerging. Steve Jobs famously looked for these tensions to innovate, leading to groundbreaking products such as the iPhone. It's a clue that there's a deeper truth to be discovered, a novel perspective to be considered. When we lean into this tension, when we dare to explore it with curiosity and courage, we often find insights hiding in the friction between conflicting viewpoints.

Consider a scenario in your organization where multiple answers are competing for the spotlight. Each side is doubling down on their position, adamant that they have the solution. The first step is to identify the question these positions are trying to answer. Perhaps one side is arguing about cost, and another is arguing about priorities. These are related issues, to be sure, but they are different frames, and the frame can make all the difference in how we see the picture.

I recall a moment when I was guest teaching in an executive education course at Harvard. After I spoke, another guest teacher arrived, and during his remarks, he vehemently (but unknowingly) contradicted some of the points I'd just made. Some students looked at me nervously, expecting it to feel awkward, but I smiled and went on listening. I recognized the value of the tension that was unfolding. It was an opportunity for the students to examine two contrasting viewpoints and arrive at their own insights.

A few of them emailed me afterwards and shared their takeaways, and just as I'd hoped, a few of them had formed their own impressions that were informed by the tension between the other teacher's perspective and mine. Even though he and I were both sharing hard-won insights from distinguished careers, they were still only partial truths to the students who needed to apply them in their own management.

For example, in the scenario above, the differing views indicate a potential gap between the market's demands and your team's capacity. Rather than viewing this as a problem, you can see it as an opportunity to foster a culture of clear communication and realistic expectation-setting within your team.

However, remember that answers are transient, only valid for the present moment and circumstances. As a leader, you must embrace adaptability. Just as seasons change, so will the circumstances around your decisions. You'll need to revisit your questions, adapt your strategies, and constantly seek out what truly matters.

Often, we find ourselves searching for a solution before we've truly understood the problem. In other words: we are trying to answer a question that we haven't fully articulated. So we need to take a step back and define the question clearly. Only then can we begin to find patterns in the cacophony of answers. This practice is particularly critical when making technology decisions because technology, so often, *is* a solution in search of a problem.

Finding Insights Amid Partial Answers

If an answer is all we seek, we may grab the first one that seems to fit and move on. But if we commit ourselves to looking for insights, we can explore the nuance in a complex situation, avoid rash decisions that may backfire, and uncover valuable wisdom that offers ongoing clarity.

Generating insights from partial answers is an art. This section offers a range of thinking tools to help you discover the insights in your partial answers.

- ◆ **Juxtaposition:** One of our most potent tools for this exercise, this allows you to take two distinctly different ideas, put them side by side, and examine what they have in common, or clarify how they differ. This practice helps us formulate profound insights that balance contrasting needs and can guide the design of solutions that incorporate both aspects harmoniously.

Suppose you're developing a health care app. You may already be aware of an inherent conflict between users' need for privacy and their desire for personalized health advice. A meaningful question shaping your work then becomes: "How can we provide personalized advice while respecting privacy?" By considering these conflicting needs, you might develop an insight such as, "Users desire personalized health advice, but not at the expense of their privacy." This could lead you to create an app that offers highly personalized advice, but that is also transparent about data usage and gives control back to the user, or that is based on anonymized data, ensuring privacy.

- **Experientially connective ideas:** Draw from your own lived experiences. They often offer valuable insights that can shape human-friendly tech decisions. This is why many start-ups spring from the frustrations faced by their founders. For example, your difficulties with city parking might inspire a service that predicts available parking. Your experience with crowded public transport could lead to a tool predicting less congested commute times.

  Now add **juxtaposition** to this set of observations and, voilà, you have an enhanced insight: many people would value comprehensive, end-to-end guidance for their commute. However, they are often limited by apps that only offer driving or transit guidance. They might be overlooking their best logistical options and could even make more sustainable choices if aspects of the experience that other apps ignore were integrated.

- **Contextual awareness:** You have a unique human advantage: you have intuitive, dimensional appreciation of all its physical, mechanical, sensory limitations and opportunities. Deeply understanding our surroundings provides a rich context that AI systems lack.

  For example, given the current remote work trend, a meaningful question you might ask could be, "How can remote workers feel more connected?" Answers may vary:

some stakeholders might suggest more video calls, others recommend less. Contextual awareness clues you in that those variances aren't just conflicting partial answers; they point to varied needs across varied teams and over the course of a real-world workday. This could drive the creation of a virtual team-building platform with a variety of ways to engage and disengage as needed.

♦ **Unrestricted creativity:** Grant yourself the freedom to get creative in ways that push your thinking in all directions. Free thinking can open up innovative insights such as imagining a world where VR is common, leading to the idea of virtual coworking spaces, or considering a world where online education is the norm, sparking the creation of VR-based learning environments.

♦ **Deep empathy:** Empathy invites us to step into the shoes of those affected by our decisions. Empathetic insights help us see beyond the numbers and statistics, beyond the charts and graphs, to the human stories that lie beneath. This is crucial for technology decision-making because an empathetic imagination can reveal where we may be introducing consequences in ways that rational analysis may overlook.

♦ **Additional considerations for examining partial answers:** There are even more lenses through which to view partial answers, such as **social responsiveness, cultural sensitivity**, and **overall ethical factors**. These considerations can guide you toward insights such as prioritizing environmental responsibility, making quality health care more accessible, amplifying mental health resources, ensuring diverse representation, or championing ethical use of AI systems.

The Synthesis Stage: Timeless Insights

Insights are the diamonds hidden in the rough of our experiences. They are timeless truths that, when considered in the current context, can guide us toward timely approaches, toward what is useful and needed right now.

Think of Apple again, and the commonly understood insight that the company uses in its strategy: that its customer base values design.

This timeless insight derives from Apple's origin story and Steve Jobs's fascination with fonts. This seemingly simple insight continues to inform their strategic choices.

But to unearth such clarifying insights, we must be willing to dig deep. They are often hidden within the tensions inherent in partial answers and the conflicts that accompany change. Tension, after all, is a sign of potential transformation. When we lean into this tension, when we approach it with curiosity and courage, we often find illuminating insights. We can also unearth foresights, which we will discuss.

Insights are like a layer of translucent film that reveals hidden text in coded messages. They help us see beyond surface-level data, to uncover truths we can apply. Most of all, they continually remind us of *what matters*. This is also what meaning does, which is how we know we're on the right track.

The process of collecting insights often involves a mix of observations, professional wisdom, and hard-learned lessons from personal experiences. The key to a future-ready decision process for meaningful transformation and innovation lies in how well we mine these insights.

Timeless Thinking with Insights

Consider a typical workday. You have a thousand thoughts competing for your attention every minute. Decisions about next quarter's sales strategy, a product defect needing immediate attention, a potential competitor entering your market, unanswered questions from your team—the list seems endless. Amid this chaos, finding time to ponder the future feels like a luxury. Yet it's a necessity.

So let's talk about the art of investing in slow thinking for timeless insights. Yes, in this fast-paced world, I will plead the case for it. I'm a big believer in carving out time for reflection and deeper thought. For instance, writing to process your thoughts can be incredibly beneficial. This technique was famously utilized by the inventor Nikola Tesla, who often wrote about his ideas before experimenting: "I do not rush into constructive work. When I get an idea, I start right away to build it up in my mind. I change the structure, I make improvements, I experiment, I run the device in my mind" (Kreutzer n.d.).

Alternatively, engaging in deep conversations can be equally valuable. Thomas Edison was known for his brainstorming sessions with his team, which led to many of his significant inventions (Vallance 2020). Even generative AI tools such as ChatGPT are handy for this sort of processing: you can assign it the role of a thoughtful conversation partner who prompts you back with follow-up questions based on what you say, and you can often dig deeper into your own thinking than you will alone.

I'm a big fan of all these approaches. Whichever of them serves you best, exploring your own mind is a leadership art. The goal is the same: to surface new thinking and uncover insights.

What Are Insights, Really?

Insights are valuable, but what *are* they, exactly? The term gets applied to different kinds of concepts at different stages of development within different industries. In the advertising world, where I have strategized campaigns for global clients, insights often refer to relevant considerations about the target audience's preferences or behaviors. However, in the broader sense, insights are more profound. They're like *aha* moments, when something you've been pondering finally clicks.

It's not just a pleasant feeling, either; lab studies in neuroscience have identified distinct brain states associated with these insights. Some people are more insight thinkers, such as Albert Einstein, known for his thought experiments, while others rely heavily on analytical thinking, such as the philosopher Rene Descartes. Cultivating intellectual curiosity, as Charles Darwin did during his voyage on the *Beagle*, can lead to more insights. Wander the world with an open mind.

You harness the fullest power of insights when you try to articulate them as part of a healthy intellectual practice. In my own work, I think of insights both as the clarifying bits of wisdom that result from synthesizing multiple conflicting partial answers *and* as the liminal holding space between the big questions you ask and the solutions on which you eventually land.

We've already examined the power of a good question; you can ask it again and again. A timeless insight, on the other hand, is something you can draw from repeatedly and find new opportunities, new approaches that are relevant and timely, that will help you to solve the problems you face in any given present moment.

The Power of Insights in Decision-Making

In decision-making, insights are the gems hidden within the data, discussions, and debates. For example, an insight about customer behavior drawn from sales data can reveal untapped market potential. These insights can spark not only clues to innovation but also empathy, accelerating our understanding. And greater understanding guides us to more informed, more sustainable decisions. Insights are the bridge that connects past learnings through present concerns into timeless guides for the future. They are nuggets of wisdom that illuminate the nuances of situations and make decisions clearer.

Using insights to make decisions is the key to exceptional strategy.

Insights, Foresights, and Empathy

Insights don't operate in isolation. They often come accompanied by foresights, those glimpses into the future that enable us to weather uncertainty with greater confidence. Together, insights and foresights help us balance the immediate needs of the now with the looming promises and vagaries of the next. They render us more adaptable, more resilient, more future-ready.

That's why insights and foresights matter. You don't have to reinvent the wheel every time you make a decision; you carry with you some wisdom about your business that you periodically refresh.

A Tool for Your Journey: The Insights Inventory

Schedule a quiet hour for reflection and make an insights inventory: a list of the insights that inform the decisions you make in your business. It's a tool that helps you uncover the underlying thoughts and beliefs that drive your actions and reactions.

You can start small and obvious, for instance, "The people who buy from us value what we offer them." However, the real value comes when you push yourself to dig deeper, to examine the underlying assumptions and tensions that inform this belief. Ask yourself:

Why do they value what you offer them? Who precisely values your offerings? What deeply truthful observations can you make about the interconnectedness of your business's success with the success of the individuals who appreciate your offerings?

Probe deeper by asking empathetic questions about the people who depend on your company: employees, customers, investors, and other stakeholders. Seek insightful guidance to understand the potential consequences of considerations currently under discussion.

When you get stuck for insights, go back and collect more questions and partial answers. You don't need to catalog every possible partial answer, but if they correspond to the viewpoint of a stakeholder, they're worth considering. In other words, say you're a food brand and a meaningful question for you is "What aspects of our product do people value the most?" It would be meaningless to answer with every ingredient, or every taste profile. But if a significant portion of your customer base have dietary issues such as allergies and that's important to them, you'll want to make sure it's listed as a partial answer.

You can keep this inventory in your working notebook or an online note-taking tool, making it accessible for revisiting whenever an additional insight occurs to you. Over time it will evolve into a powerful tool, continually reminding you how to act from your core sense of purpose.

The Context Mapping Stage: Context, Externalities, and Trends

Once we've gathered these insights, we can begin to look at them within the bigger picture—**contexts**, **externalities**, and **trends**. These elements help shape useful and **timely approaches** and workable answers to the original question, or a reframed question.

But the process doesn't stop there. By looking at this broader context, we can often begin to anticipate future trends and develop **bankable foresights**—educated guesses about what may matter in the future.

Monitoring and Understanding External Trends

One way to ensure you're seeing as far ahead as you need to is to regularly shift your gaze from internal operations to external happenings. Broadly speaking, pay attention to what's happening now. The trends happening in culture are patterns that, when viewed at the right angle, can provide clues about where society may be heading.

For example, there have been indicators about gender trends for a good many years now. Futurist and author Faith Popcorn identified a cultural trend about gender fluidity at least as far back as 2016. We're seeing that bear out in the rise of gender-free clothing and bathrooms, increasing amount of identity discourse, and focus on transgender and nonbinary individuals and rights.

Trends as Bankable Foresights

Noticing a trend does not necessarily mean immediate action. It could become a bankable foresight—a development that is anticipated to be significant but does not require immediate action. If you were a fashion designer, recognizing the gender fluidity trend when Faith pointed it out would have been beneficial. It might have become part of your longer-range thinking and planning, a data point along your strategic road map.

Tracking Externalities

In terms of externalities, what are you keeping an eye on that's beyond your control but stands to have a great impact on your business?

These are worth your time to monitor. Look for:

- **Measurability:** Can the impact of these external factors be quantified?
- **Changes:** What methods are you using to track the likelihood that it changes?
- **Tipping points:** How will you know when the situation has reached a tipping point?
- **Experimentation:** What small steps could you take to be well versed in the trend and stay ahead of these changes?
- **Long-term planning:** How far into the future can you forecast potential changes, and when might these changes occur?

The Decision Point Stage: Timely Actions and Bankable Foresights

Yes, I hear you; you need solutions *now*. That's where the beauty of the insights-foresights model shines. It allows you to deal with the demands of the present while keeping an eye on the future. Once you've begun to use the process, you can move faster with greater confidence. This model is grounded in timeless insights—which, again, are universal truths that remain relevant *regardless* of the changing landscape—while also incorporating timely, time-bound approaches and answers that address current realities. By balancing these elements, we can develop foresight, allowing us to visualize outcomes—both good and bad—and prepare accordingly, even if we don't need to put those foresights to immediate use. I call these little bonuses *"bankable foresights."* We can, in a sense, *bank* them for later.

But in doing so, you accumulate wisdom. Foresights, after all, are not just about predicting the future; they're about preparing a path for it. They help us anticipate future trends—what may matter later—and set up to be ready for them. This requires a blend of strategic optimism and pragmatic realism. Foresights are like the North Star: they might not illuminate our immediate surroundings, but they provide a point of reference toward which we can navigate. Foresights answer the questions "What could happen next?" and "How should we prepare for it?" By understanding current trends and historical patterns, you can make educated guesses about the future and position yourself to seize opportunities when they arise.

For example, in a recent consulting project with a major retailer, we helped them determine the future-readiness of one of their product lines. They needed to decide whether the platform they were invested in would still be mainstream within a few years. By asking questions that framed the right sort of viewpoint and looking at relevant trend reports and financial indicators, we were able to make confident recommendations to give them a competitive edge.

The Beauty of Bankable Foresights

Bankable foresights are the most valuable wisdom you'll develop in this process. They are those nuggets of potential future reality that we can "bank" for later use: you can set them aside and not have to act on them today, but proceed with confidence knowing you have a clearer idea of what the future may hold. Bankable foresights most likely won't change our immediate course of action, but they should inform our long-term strategy. They ensure our alignment from now to the future through our next course of action.

Insights Inform Foresights

Both insight and foresight are essential for effective problem-solving. By using both, we can not only find solutions to the problems we're facing today, but also anticipate and prevent problems that might otherwise arise in the future.

Insight is a function of time, tension, and context. It's a way of looking at the world that allows us to find guiding truths. It's a tool that we can all benefit from using, whether we're working on a personal project or a professional one.

Foresight is the ability to see an aspect of the future to anticipate potential problems, opportunities, or change overall. It's a way of thinking that allows us to be proactive rather than reactive.

There are many ways to develop foresight, but one of the most important is to always be on the lookout for insights. By constantly being on the lookout for those *aha* moments, we can start to see patterns and trends that others might miss. We can begin to understand how the world is changing and what might happen next.

Insight and foresight are two sides of the same coin. Insight helps us understand the present so that we can anticipate the future. Foresight helps us see the potential consequences of our actions and make decisions accordingly.

Bonus Step: Using AI for Brainstorming

You might want to consider generative AI as a helpful "colleague" here—one who can sift through mountains of data in seconds but still needs your human judgment to make sense of it all. It can be tireless in question-and-answer sessions, allowing you to reframe your thinking until you get the breakthrough you need. This balance between AI processing and human insight is where we can make magic happen.

Circling Back

From uncertainty to questions, from insights to foresights, the insights-foresights model is a powerful tool for navigating the complexities of our too-fast world.

This is not about having all the answers. You never will. Navigating the unknown is part of the leadership journey. But even uncertainty is no match for a good questions-and-insights session. The thing about uncertainty is once you begin trying to articulate those big unasked questions, everything becomes less daunting. You can begin to build a framework around what you don't know and start learning.

We can equip ourselves with the courage to ask meaningful questions as well as the intellectual honesty to remain curious through initial rounds of partial answers until we arrive at powerful insights and bankable foresights. That creates spaces for reflection and dialogue, where diverse perspectives are heard and respected. It fosters a mindset of exploration and experimentation, where failure is seen not as a setback but as a steppingstone toward better insights.

Remember: insights don't always come in flashes of brilliance. More often, they emerge slowly, subtly, in the quiet moments of reflection, in the thoughtful exchanges of ideas, in the patient observation of patterns. They require us to slow down, to listen, to observe, to question. They call us to be mindful, present, attentive.

So, as you think about your next strategic decision, ask yourself: What are your insights telling you? What are your bankable foresights? And most importantly, what meaningful questions are you asking to get started?

Data, Insights, and Intuition

Executives often trust their instincts over data, and given their experience, they're often right—both because rising to executive leadership has indeed generally proceeded from having good instincts, and because the data available to work with might be limited and misleading.

However, this doesn't mean we couldn't make better decisions with better data. Data, in its raw form, provides partial answers—only you very often don't know the questions it's attempting to answer.

To unlock its full potential, we need to either determine what question the existing data is answering, or, ideally, obtain the data that answers the most meaningful question we know to ask.

And here's the thing: intuition can guide us in identifying that distinction! The goal isn't to prioritize data over intuition or vice versa, but to have them work in harmony, solving the same problem.

The more we rely on data to make decisions, the more we need insights to complement the data. It's too easy to look at abstracted data as numbers and graphs without remembering the people that data represents. The insights we bring to the analysis of our data remind us what stories we're looking for in the data, and what foresights we might find.

The Deceptive Duality of Data

Data can be a powerful tool for decision-making, but how do you make sure the data you have is trustworthy? After all, data alone isn't enough. Data is just measurement, but you can set up metrics for anything, and it doesn't mean that they're meaningful. Data can lead you astray.

There are two common pitfalls: false equivalencies and cherry-picking.

False Equivalencies: Correlation versus Causation

False equivalencies occur when we mistake correlation for causation. We might assume that because two things rise and fall together, one caused the other.

For instance, ice cream sales and swimming pool drownings both increase in hot weather, but one doesn't cause the other. Similarly, correlation between church donations and liquor sales doesn't imply causation; both simply increase when the economy is doing well.

Just because two things are correlated, doesn't mean that one caused the other.

Still, a lot more of our decisions than we'd care to admit are based in ice-cream-drowning and church-drinking sort of thinking.

It's a common misconception to equate correlation with causation, a fallacy that can result in misguided decisions—especially when an inaccurate reading of the data would support your initial hypothesis and lead you to double down on the wrong factor.

It happens a lot in tech-driven experiences.

And sometimes those false equivalencies lead us to miss opportunities to remove harmful presumptions from our products.

Cherry-Picking: Seeing What We Want to See

Cherry-picking is subtly deceptive. It occurs when we look only at the data supporting our argument, ignoring the rest. Like a prosecutor building a case, we might be tempted to ignore data that doesn't align with our narrative. For instance, if we focus only on the high sales of a recently launched product, we might miss the bigger picture—that overall company sales have declined. To avoid this, when we're looking at data, we need to ask whether there's any other possible interpretation. If there is, you might be looking at a case of cherry-picking. We need to consider the big picture and to be aware of other factors that could be affecting the data you're looking at.

With cherry-picking comes the risk of cannibalizing, which is a rather unpleasant term for when one product line "eats" into the opportunity for other products.

I'll share an example.

At one point in my career, I was managing the renewals business for Magazines.com. I was also managing their email program. The company had historically pushed hard in every channel to sell cheap *People* magazine subscriptions because they were viewed as loss leaders that would get customers in the door, but something wasn't working out right in the equation. There were too many cancellations as the first terms were coming up for renewal.

Eventually a colleague and I crunched enough numbers to work out what was happening: customers were buying the cheap first-term subscriptions in lieu of a steeper-priced renewal (where the company hoped to make its money back). We also saw why. When the subscribers to *People* were getting their renewal notices by email, those emails often had cross-sell promotions—including, sometimes, for *People*. We were doing nothing to exclude those promotions for first-term rates from the renewal emails. That meant that we were losing revenue *and* causing customer confusion about the right course of action, so even though customers were getting a deal, it wasn't a great experience, and it could have ultimately meant a decrease in their satisfaction and loyalty. Once we added programming logic to the renewal emails to exclude promotions for the title being renewed, cancellations went down and renewals went up.

It meant taking a small hit in the reporting metrics of our $1 M/yr email channel but restoring the stability of our $10 M/yr renewals program. And if I remember correctly, it meant a net gain of about $1 million a year across all channels. It seems easy to recognize in retrospect, but it is this holistic way of thinking about the entire business model and how it is presented to every customer, one by one, that makes it work in the details.

Trustworthy Data

To navigate the complexities of tech acceleration, we must understand what "meaningful" really means: what matters, what is important. It requires adopting a scientific mindset to interpret data and insights effectively and developing well-thought-out ideas. Once a promising idea emerges, the challenge becomes communicating its value and leading effectively through times of change.

In *Think Again*, Adam Grant describes our thinking roles as the preacher, the prosecutor, and the professor. At times, we persuade ourselves and others like a preacher, or build a case like a prosecutor. Other times, we analyze data like a professor, seeking lessons. Our role shifts depending on the situation. But to lead with integrity, we must base our decisions on the best information.

Measure and Anticipate

The success of this model hinges on the idea that meaning is about what matters, and innovation is about what is likely to matter. Here I will add that an important dimension to acting on this overall insight is to measure what matters to you and your business. Or at least to get as close as you possibly can.

As stated in the 2009 Report by the Commission on the Measurement of Economic Performance and Social Progress, "What we measure affects what we do; and if our measurements are flawed, decisions may be distorted" (CMEPSP n.d.).

We also want to find a way to keep an eye on what is going to matter. Is there a metric, a study? Trust is one of the important elements in the work I do. Public relations company Edelman does a study every year, so I keep an eye on their reporting. I also track the idea of risk. The World Economic Forum publishes a risk report every year. These are wheels I don't need to reinvent. I can follow their observations, as peripheral to my own thinking, and glean what I need from them. You may need to use proxy measures, but it's important that they're telling you something directional that can meaningfully influence your decision-making.

Ethical Decision-Making in an AI-Led World

A world increasingly driven by algorithms and AI systems presents unique challenges in ethical decision-making. The stakes are high—our decisions can engage or alienate users, bring benefits, or cause unintended harm. In this context, the process of decision-making must be deeply reflective, strategic, and, above all, human centered.

Balancing Optimization and User Needs

Consider an instance where you're deciding how to tweak the gamification strategy of a series of push notifications to engage users. You know that at a certain level of frequency, these alerts bring users back to the platform. But you also know that too many push notifications will backfire. Users will disable the notifications on their devices, or worse yet, disable notifications, cancel their service, or even delete their accounts. You risk alienating them, *and* you also risk contributing to a cycle of addiction.

Or take the case of Duolingo, the popular language-learning platform, as an example. Their decision to introduce AI-led personalized learning paths was a game changer. However, the decision wasn't just about using the latest AI technology. It was about understanding their users and their individual learning needs. They asked the right questions: How can AI enhance the learning experience? How can it cater to the diverse learning styles of our users?

The Limits of AI Systems in Decision-Making

AI tools can provide some assistance when it comes to decision-making, in certain very specific ways. If you take a question such as "How can we grow the business without spending a lot more cash in the immediate term" and pose it to a large language model such as ChatGPT, one thing you can count on for sure is that you will get an answer. It might not be a deeply insightful answer, but it will be an answer formulated from statistically likely words. And for some purposes that is extremely useful and a great time saver. I've used LLM tools every day for years to help me gain efficiency.

Large language model chatbots such as ChatGPT can help you quickly iterate through the questions-insights-foresights process, challenging your own thinking and arriving at a rich set of partial answers that can lead to insights—if we don't rely too literally on their feedback. Because what machine learning models *don't* do is vast when it comes to knowledge work and executive insights. They don't understand context, trends, the marketplace, your culture, the experiments you've tried and abandoned, or countless other factors that would make the feedback more valuable and hence, more meaningful.

That's why when the fashion retailer Stitch Fix harnessed the power of AI, such as machine learning, to provide personalized style recommendations, they recognized that AI alone can't capture the nuances of personal style. So they incorporated human stylists in their decision-making process, combining machine efficiency with human intuition.

Machines do a lot of things well, but one of the things AI systems can't do is make things meaningful to humans. For that we need actual humans. Because when we're making decisions that affect human experience, what we're looking for are human insights.

Implications across Sectors

For the sake of clarity, I've compiled some examples from real-life feedback from clients, with all identifying information removed. But the breadth of considerations should still illustrate how faceted human-friendly tech decision-making needs to be.

For instance, perhaps your HR department wants to implement an AI-powered hiring system to streamline the recruitment process. You know that this could help you review more candidates than you might otherwise see. But what if the algorithm isn't properly trained and introduces bias?

Perhaps you work in transportation, and you'd like to expand the use of facial recognition technology in security and surveillance. You know that passengers can get through lines faster, but you also know that this could infringe on individual privacy rights and be misused for mass surveillance by authorities.

In manufacturing, perhaps you want to integrate more automation and robotics to boost productivity. You know that this could result in greater efficiencies for the company and greater safety for the workers on the floor. But you also know that this could result in job losses and economic disruption for workers in the affected industries.

Even in a mobile app, let's say you want to launch a new feature such as an "infinite scroll" or push notifications. While these might enhance user engagement, they could also have unintended and unforeseen psychological impacts, leading to increased screen time and reduced productivity.

The right decisions in AI-led environments will require a careful balance of evaluating technological benefits and potential risks to human experiences and societal norms.

Decision Tool: Building to Bankable Foresights

1. What insights can you glean from partial answers?

Analyze initial responses for insights.

2. What trends and context should be considered?

Review relevant trends, externalities, and the broader context.

3. What foresights can you anticipate and set aside?

Identify foresights to "bank"—insights that guide and calibrate your actions without needing immediate execution.

CHAPTER 4

Through-Line Thinking
Ethical Impacts and Beyond

The glaring demands of the present are often at odds with the still-hazy realm of the future. We're tasked with making decisions that propel us forward along a tightrope between "what matters now" and "what is likely to matter." In fact, effective leadership rests on a tenuous balancing act of action and inaction. Both must be carefully considered. Overstep our understanding with reckless action, and we risk causing unintended harm. Hesitate, and you may lose market share, fall into irrelevance, or, indeed, cause harm.

In our too-fast world accelerated by technology, balance becomes ever more challenging. AI systems and automation ratchet up the scale and speed of our decisions. And that in turn amplifies the potential consequences.

The Harms of Action vs. the Harms of Inaction
Harm can result from biases toward either action or inaction. The action bias can lead us to act even when there may be no evidence that will lead to a better outcome than doing nothing (Pilat and Krastev n.d.). Conversely, the status quo bias can lead to inaction even when change is needed (see Figure 4.1).

As the now-next continuum helps us understand how actions and decisions connect across time, it also plots the escalating harms of inaction toward the past and the growing harms of action toward

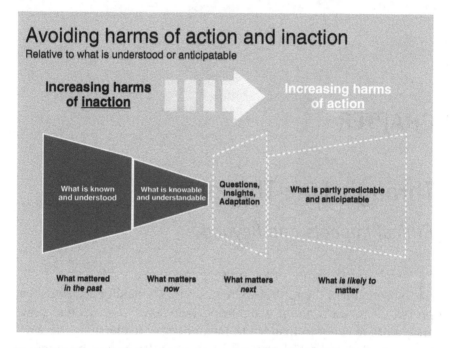

Figure 4.1 Harms of action and inaction along the now–next continuum.

the future. This illustrates that delaying action on something known to cause harm increases the harms of inaction. Conversely, when we rush to release products or technologies that reach beyond our understanding of their implications and consequences, we increase the harms of action.

Throughout emerging technology, we can see examples of products that exceed our understanding of potential consequences. Facial recognition technology, for example, has incredible potential as a time-savings and convenience, with the ability to offer targeted experiences for people across a range of applications. But biometric information such as our faces and fingerprints are some of our most challenging privacy constraints. Unlike passwords, we can't change them. And unfortunately, many facial recognition applications have demonstrated that they are trained on biased data that puts people disproportionately at risk. Black- and brown-skinned people are frequently misidentified. When facial recognition is used in surveillance systems for law enforcement, this discrepancy can have severe, life-altering, and society-damaging consequences. This is a classic example of the harms of action—we have run too far ahead without gaining sufficient insights, and people too often suffer as a result.

On the other end of the spectrum, I've seen companies delay necessary changes, clinging to outdated systems and processes due to fear of the unknown. The most evident and damaging category of these harms is climate change: companies whose products contribute to carbon emissions without invoking a sustainable plan for mitigation are often either running out the clock or kicking the can down the road. The longer we delay acting on something that we know is causing harm, the more we invoke the harms of inaction.

Existing Models for Ethical Decision Making
We aren't going to explore the fullness of what philosophy and ethics have to say on these matters, but it's worth noting that frameworks such as deontology and utilitarianism exist and can be useful in understanding how we navigate the decision-making process. Deontology, for example, aligns with the principle "first, do no harm." A core principle of deontological ethics asserts that all individuals have inherent value and should be treated with respect and consideration. Utilitarianism, meanwhile, maintains a steady focus on consequences and outcomes.

In brief, consider this scenario: you're considering rolling out a conversational chatbot for customer support. Deploying it at scale might put hundreds of customer support representatives out of work, but it will save the company money and help prepare for future expansion.

If the chatbot could save the company money, improve efficiency, and prepare for future expansion, a utilitarian might argue that deploying the chatbot is the best course of action, despite the potential job loss for current customer service representatives.

On the other hand, if deploying the chatbot would result in hundreds of customer service representatives losing their jobs, a deontologist might argue against deploying the chatbot, viewing the job loss as a harmful action that should be avoided.

This gets a little more confusing, though: at least one analysis suggests that sometimes when people choose inaction, they are *rejecting the assumptions* of the possible action. This challenges the idea that deontological and utilitarian responses are naturally opposed (Baron and Goodwin 2020). And it muddies the waters a bit for us. Besides, for many people, these models are already too complex and abstract to be of much use in practical decision-making.

While not the same as the models used in ethics and philosophy, I intend the harms of action and harms of inaction to be a simpler model for people to understand. In facilitating future-readiness discussions with clients, I have seen that, for many people, these concepts make ethical considerations much clearer. And if the ethics of the choices become clearer, there's a better chance that people will make better choices.

Through-Line Thinking: Working through Past Actions to Understand the Future

To understand the harms of either action or inaction, we begin by understanding that not only does our direction matter, but so does the size of our steps. If we stride too far too quickly, we risk overstepping our understanding and potentially causing harm. Conversely, if our steps are too small, too timid, we risk lagging behind, missing out on growth opportunities, unable to harness the potential benefits technology offers.

So we need an approach to thinking that is lucid enough to see our actions, decisions, and outcomes as interconnected, not just in the present but extending into the future. That's the essence of through-line thinking, a way of modeling actions and decisions so that they connect from the past to the outcomes of today and tomorrow in a continuous thread (see Figure 4.2).

The answer lies in finding the right balance relative to the harms presented by the circumstances. We must be swift in adapting, but not at the cost of thorough consideration and strategic planning. Our actions must be driven by relentless strategy and empathy, allowing us to leverage technological advancements in a manner that serves humanity while keeping us competitive in the marketplace. And we must consider the continuity of our actions.

As a consultant, I've had the privilege of guiding clients to applying through-line thinking to a diverse array of decisions along the

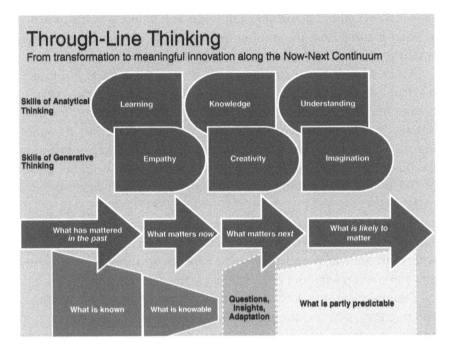

Figure 4.2 Skills of through-line thinking.

now-next continuum. During these collaborations, we've both come to an even deeper realization that decision-making is not about choosing in isolation. The key to making complex projects work lies in the flow of decisions we have made collectively in the past, the realities of the present, and the visions we hold for the future.

Let's consider a company embarking on an exciting AI project. The technology is new and has exciting prospects, yet it raises ethical questions about data privacy. The leadership could choose to charge ahead, prioritizing innovation and market share over unclear ethics. But in applying through-line thinking, they consider the long-term impact of such a decision. Could it erode trust with their users? Could it set a dangerous precedent for data misuse? In the end, perhaps they decide to pause the project and invest incrementally in technologies with more robust privacy measures.

At its core, through-line thinking helps us comprehend that now and next are not rival entities. They are parts of a continuum not only of time but of *knowledge*. It steers us from questions through insights to foresights, from imagination to understanding and through to imagination again. The power of through-line thinking helps us arrive at what matters next by guiding us from what is knowable to what is partly predictable, building a through line that connects the dots.

More than a single strategy, through-line thinking is a mindset. It's an awareness of how decisions resonate through time, creating echoes that reverberate into the future. It's choosing not just for now, but also for the possible opportunities you may shape. It's recognizing that the actions and decisions you've already taken are tied to the outcomes of today and tomorrow—which leaves you more aware of the power and potential of the actions and decisions you will make today.

Through-line thinking helps us ask questions today that help surface the insights we'll need to shape tomorrow. We can do this with both analytical and generative aspects. In other words, sometimes you're anticipating consequences through the skills of analytical thinking: learning, knowledge, and understanding. At other times you might engage the complementary skills of generative thinking to anticipate consequences: empathy, creativity, and imagination. We're responsible for following our thinking through from end to end, even if we act from step to step.

You can align these against a sense of time and recurring cycles of assessment and decision-making. At each point that you stop to consider what matters, you are looking backward and forward, trying to use the collected set of thinking skills to paint a clearer picture of what you need to plan for.

Ecosystem Effects and Through-Line Thinking

Your organization doesn't operate in a vacuum. Understanding the broader ecosystem—the people, the communities, the environment—affected by your operations is vital. Take Airbnb, criticized for its impact on neighborhoods and housing markets. A deeper consideration of the ecosystem and better through-line thinking could have prompted proactive measures, benefiting not just Airbnb but also the communities they operate within.

Many decisions, particularly in the context of rapidly evolving, technology-driven spaces, are a tug-of-war between the potential harms of action and inaction. Through many intricate discussions with leaders and innovators I have come to realize that these decisions most often are not about harm avoidance but about choosing which harm we must confront and how we will mitigate the risks. And we must make these choices in full awareness of the larger context of our surrounding ecosystems. This kind of systems thinking around ecosystem effects asks us to view our decisions and actions through a wider, more encompassing lens. It complements through-line thinking, understanding that our actions ripple out, touching various parts of the ecosystem (see Figure 4.3). It means zooming out to see the bigger picture, understanding the broader impacts, and making more informed, thoughtful choices.

Misalignment and Consequences at Scale

The sugarcane industry in Hawaii in the 1800s had a rat problem. They were damaging crops. Plantation owners heard about the success Jamaica and other Caribbean islands had had in using the

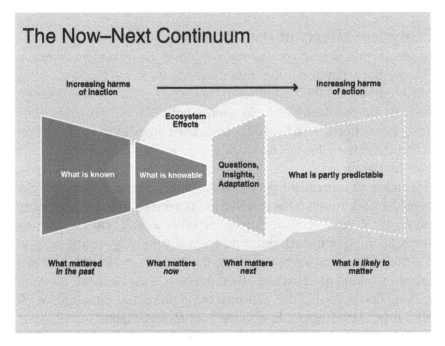

Figure 4.3 The now–next continuum and ecosystem effects.

mongoose to control rats, so in the late nineteenth century, they decided to import mongooses to Hawaii as well.

Between 1883 and 1885, mongooses were brought from Jamaica and released in the sugarcane fields on the Big Island, Maui, and Oahu.

There was just one critical detail no one considered. Mongooses and rats have different activity patterns: mongooses are diurnal—active during the day—and rats are nocturnal. The mongooses, then, had little impact on the rat population. They likely had had no impact on the rats in Jamaica, either, but took the credit even as plantations changed the way they managed crops and made more profit. What the mongooses did, however, do was devastate the populations of native Hawaiian birds and sea turtles. To this day, the introduction of the mongoose to Hawaii is considered one of the most damaging invasive species introductions. And it is a fantastically unfortunate example of consequences at scale that were not anticipated but probably could have been. Perhaps you've heard the story before. But what insights does it offer us about technology and human experience?

Ecosystem Effects in Tech Decisions

Implementing a new technology will affect its immediate users, of course. But what about the wider societal impacts? The ripples that reach far beyond the boardroom? Through-line thinking encourages us to tackle problem-solving in a more holistic way, conscious of the ecosystem effects. This broader perspective urges us to come up with comprehensive solutions that tackle the root causes of problems, not just the symptoms.

Rather than treat all decisions as binary choices, we can often consider opportunities for iterative improvement. This method, a cornerstone of agile methodologies, involves taking small, measured steps, learning from each one, and gradually moving toward the goal.

This isn't about creeping along timidly. It's about informed progression, taking the next step, then the next, then the next. It's about making decisions that don't surpass our current understanding, while always being ready to adapt as we gain more insights.

Unintended or Unanticipated? Unexpected or Unforeseen?

In a 1936 essay titled "The Unanticipated Consequences of Purposive Social Action," Robert K. Merton, a renowned American sociologist, introduced the concept of "unanticipated consequences" as part of a framework for analyzing different types of consequences that may arise from deliberate actions, which were not intended or foreseen. The three types of effects included:

1. **Perverse results:** Outcomes that are the opposite of what was intended or expected.
2. **Unexpected drawbacks:** Undesirable and unforeseen side effects that accompany the intended result.
3. **Unforeseen benefits:** Positive consequences that were not anticipated or planned for.

Merton's use of "unanticipated" rather than "unintended" was deliberate and significant. "Unanticipated" refers to consequences that were not predicted or foreseen, while "unintended" implies consequences that were not the original objective. Over time, however, these two terms have become conflated and used interchangeably, obscuring the nuanced distinction Merton intended to make (Botsman 2022). While "unintended consequences" is the term most used to discuss amplified outcomes such as bias in tech, it's worth noting the through-line thinking in Merton's classification. Whatever terms we use, it's important to think through the consequences that flow from our decisions.

Perverse Incentives

Back when I ran an agency that specializes in experience optimization, we frequently ran A/B and multivariate tests to improve conversion rate and customer retention on client websites and marketing channels. Every so often, a client would propose that we charge them based on a percentage of the lift we brought to their channels or to the site. But we had explored this opportunity from the outset and found that it introduced *perverse incentives*—in other words, motivations that don't align between stakeholders. In this case, the arrangement might have tempted us (even subconsciously) to bolster our efforts artificially, or at the expense of other campaigns that we weren't managing. In the short term, my company may have made a tidy fortune from this arrangement, but over time, we would have become a very different culture, driven by very different metrics, and I valued our integrity. These kinds of misaligned motivations are common ethical quagmires.

Tech Mongooses

Numerous experiences with technology projects that overlooked aspects of human impacts have taught me a valuable lesson. The "best" decision isn't always the most technologically advanced or the most financially lucrative. It's usually the decision that takes into consideration most aspects of the situation, including what it means for the humans involved. It's the decision that aligns with our values, serves our purpose, and contributes to a better future. This is why foresight is indispensable in tech decisions.

If our tendency to view the future in dystopian terms serves any useful purpose, it is to keep us honest about what we fear and what we'd like to avoid. Most people agree that a hostile robot takeover, as we see so often in sci-fi, is not what we would wish for. That's easy to see and acknowledge. But the less alarmist and more likely versions of bad outcomes are often more subtle, more specific to a subset of people, and given to exponential effects, where we tend not to see them until they're causing big problems.

Algorithmic bias, such as what has been documented within hiring systems, credit card approvals, search results, and so much else, are like this. Very often they disproportionately affect one or a few groups of people. Most people don't know when this is happening. Even people affected by this bias don't always know when it's happening.

For instance, consider the use of algorithms in loan approval processes. These could favor applicants from wealthy postal codes— even inadvertently, based on years of biased historical data being used for training—which would further marginalize certain lower-income demographic groups. On top of that, the output from the algorithm might not be readily transparent or explainable, which would make remediation far more challenging.

But that's just the tip of the iceberg. The implications reach into depths we're only beginning to explore. There are countless examples of unanticipated consequences when our decisions reach a vast scale, causing harms that we did not foresee. But like the diurnal mongoose and the nocturnal rat: Are the consequences so elusive? If we ask better questions and examine the likely outcomes, how many more disastrous outcomes could we avoid?

From sourcing limited datasets to embedding biased decisions into algorithmic processes, the state of AI is full of unfortunate starting points. The problems are there already, and we must do the best we can. But that doesn't mean we should import new problems that will turn into even bigger nightmares.

As a leader, as a thinker, as someone who takes responsibility for shaping the future we want to create, how do you avoid getting this wrong?

By now we know that we cultivate foresight by asking meaningful questions. Questions that challenge us, that push us to think differently, that open us up to new perspectives. Questions such as: What if we tried this? What could go wrong? What could go right? Who would benefit? Who could be harmed?

These questions don't always have easy answers. They're not meant to. They're meant to provoke thought, to stimulate discussion, to spark insights. They're meant to guide us, not toward a predetermined destination, but toward a deeper consideration of what matters and what could matter next.

And to remind us: We're not alone. Our actions do not take place in isolation. We're part of a community, a society, a world. Our decisions affect others, and their decisions affect us. We're interconnected and interdependent.

As we make decisions, we do well to listen to others, learn from their experiences, and share our own; to collaborate, cooperate, and cocreate. How might we share ownership of the process—especially within communities of people who will be affected by the decisions you make? How can we foster an environment where everyone not only feels seen, heard, and valued but can also contribute their unique perspective toward collective wisdom? Someone you involve in the discussion and decision process might even have the fore-sight to notice when something that looks to someone else like a solution—like mongooses—may turn into a bigger problem.

Misconceptions About Ethics Meet the AI Age

There's a longstanding misconception that ethics are only there to impede development and progress—to throw cold water on hot, bright, shiny new ideas, and ruin all the fun. This couldn't be further from the truth.

During my career, I've seen firsthand as ethical considerations play out in practice. For example, while working as a business ana-lyst for enterprise-level companies, my role was to gather a set of requirements, from user needs to business constraints. This often presented me with serious limitations that needed addressing. For instance, a hospital with facilities to treat only two critical heart patients at once forced us to examine our ethical responsibility in prioritizing care. In another case, an accounting system synchronized with an external data feed only once a week, so it might have inad-vertently disadvantaged certain stakeholders throughout the week, raising questions about the fairness of the process.

In this context, then, ethical considerations are not roadblocks but guardrails. They keep us safe as we speed along the too-fast highway of innovation. When we integrate ethics into our decision-making process, we avoid costly mistakes, prevent serious harms, and garner valuable insights.

It benefits every organization to have an "ethical north'"—a clear statement of ethical commitments and values that guides decision-making like a compass. Google's former motto, "Don't be evil," served this purpose (until they removed it from its place of prominence in their code of conduct in 2018). Your ethical north should influence your starting point on critical decisions, such as your stance on data privacy, a hot-button issue today.

When executed correctly, ethical processes act like requirements gathering. They coax out into the open the unspoken details of systemic context or the practical limitations that are often too easily overlooked.

Through a strong starting point and the process of ethical "requirements gathering," ethics in practice offer a setting for honest, high-integrity conversations. These dialogues make it easier to investigate constraints and limitations as well as opportunities and progress since we're more likely to be talking about the same issues using the same language.

Demystifying How We Talk and Think About AI

I've seen many buzzwords come and go throughout my years as a Tech Humanist. But few have been as misunderstood, and as consequential, as artificial intelligence.

For decades, artificial intelligence has for most people been an abstraction that computer enthusiasts were excited about, and the general population mostly knew about it through movies. And the people were nervous.

To be sure, by the very name and nature of "artificial intelligence" it has always promised much. Until recently it has delivered little. AI has now become a ubiquitous presence in our lives, and certainly in the headlines. To listen to the media narrative, either AI will kill us all, or it will be what transforms our existence. The extreme scenarios are indeed both exhilarating and terrifying, long on visions of unprecedented advancements while simultaneously raising existential concerns about its potential and current harms.

What we tend to lump together as "AI" in everyday discussions is not in fact one single technology. When we gather around conference tables or join video calls to discuss "AI," we're often not talking about the same thing. Artificial intelligence, a term coined in the 1960s and loaded with plenty of unintended and unforeseen consequences of its own since its inception, is effectively a marketing term for a category of technologies, rather than a clear label of one specific technology.

Huddled together under that umbrella, for example, you'll find a variety of **machine learning (ML)** approaches. Many of these have been around a while and are by now the workhorses of our digital world. We've all experienced them, knowingly or not, in spam filters, recommendation engines, and credit scoring, to name just a few examples. They function by combining data, statistical models, and algorithms such that human involvement isn't necessary—although sometimes humans still are involved, especially when reviewing decisions and recommendations made by ML.

Then there's **deep learning**. If this kind of AI were a person, it would wear a dark velvet cloak. This is machine learning, too, but based on neural networks modeled after the human brain. It deduces patterns from large datasets, working its magic in speech recognition or in computer vision, which we commonly experience as facial recognition, but also, for example, plays a big role in self-driving vehicles and medical diagnosis. This is the tech I often think of when I remember Arthur C. Clarke's third law: "Any sufficiently advanced technology is indistinguishable from magic." It *isn't* magic, of course, but it's a category of technology that in application often *feels* like it.

Another useful distinction to be aware of is between **supervised learning** and **unsupervised learning**. Supervised learning is what happens whenever you train a model on a sufficiently large set of examples that have a value one way or the other, like credit card fraud detection (i.e. this one is fraud, this one isn't, etc.) or image recognition (e.g. this one is a cat, this one isn't, etc.). Unsupervised learning, again, feels a bit magic-adjacent: it's when a model reviews a broad and unlabeled dataset, such as customer data, and discerns patterns that would have been impossible or at least difficult for humans to notice, such as segments based on obscure characteristics. Deep learning can be either supervised or unsupervised (or semi-supervised).

There's also **reinforcement learning**, which is often used in gaming, robotics—from your vacuum cleaner to a picker on the Amazon warehouse floor, and even self-driving vehicles. In this approach, the model is basically set loose to conduct its own experiments trying to navigate and determine its own rules for an environment it is trying to make sense of. It may be rewarded for taking certain paths, which may encourage it to find the path of least resistance. It may find weird ways of getting to the goal: for example, climbing walls.

Janelle Shane describes some strange and hilarious experiments with reinforcement learning in her 2018 book *You Look Like a Thing and I Love You: How Artificial Intelligence Works and Why It's Making the World a Weirder Place*. (Gotta be in the top-five best book titles of all time.)

From an ethics and responsible tech perspective, one of the challenges of the models that feels the most like magic is that it's harder to interpret how they arrived at their decisions and patterns. Interpretability is one of the attributes of ethical AI most called for by ethics and policy experts. But by these models' very nature they are designed to determine their own patterns from large datasets, and they do so through massive volumes of math and decisions nested upon decisions. That's less of a problem with machine learning models based on decision trees and more structured sets of rules.

The might-as-well-be-magic these systems stand to offer in shaping the future of human experiences is significant. In terms of the "what matters" and "what is likely to matter" of it all, this is where the rubber meets the road.

On some level unless you're a data scientist or an engineer these distinctions make little difference. But as the world around us is shaped more and more by AI-informed experiences—and as we are more and more able to determine how to utilize AI in our own decision-making—it matters that we have some familiarity with the overall picture.

Another important facet to the AI discussion that's important is that of AGI, or artificial general intelligence. Broadly, that's the notion of a machine intelligence equal to or better than humans at pretty much everything. Much debate consumes experts about the definition and the potential timeline of whatever we agree to call AGI. But experts are nowhere near in agreement that AGI is even plausible in the near term. There's this notion that in talking about the adoption of artificial intelligence we're talking about artificial general intelligence. But that's simply not true in this era, and it's not likely to be true any time soon.

Clearly AI can already out-math us, and it can write much faster than we can, although that doesn't necessarily mean the output is better. But can it do *everything* we can? C'mon—*sarcasm*? That's probably going to take a minute. *Empathy* might take a bit longer.

Does it matter? Even when generalized AI can do nearly everything we can do at generally the same level or better, what does that prove? What does it imply? Do we simply hand over the keys and say, "AI, take the wheel"?

That probably doesn't make sense, it probably isn't necessary, and it probably isn't wise. So why do so many of us have our eye on that arbitrary line of demarcation?

Most of the AI we need to discuss and decide on is specialized. It's a set of data and rules that pertain to a particular field, such as loan approvals, spam filtering, image recognition, and yes, text generation. In general, an AI that specializes in one of those tasks is not going to be very good at any of the others.

So when we think about how AI can disrupt our industry, transform our business, and lead to innovative new solutions, most of the time we need to be thinking specialized. And that again points to the need to be dialed in on what problem you're trying to solve and whom you solve it for: all those classic questions of strategy and marketing and product development.

It's a tool, and its value is in how we use it, but it's also a degree removed from that: a tool that we're building *to help coordinate us*. It's that level of abstraction that requires significant consideration of how our own mental tools work.

Knowing Our Own Minds

Humans have incredible brains. They're a significant part of what sets us apart from other animals, and it's these brains that have inspired the design and evolution of artificial intelligence. But unlike those nonhuman animals and AI "peers," we are capable of abstract reasoning in ways those minds are not (yet). Our brains enable us in essence to time travel mentally so that we can relive past experiences and imagine future scenarios. Our sophisticated language abilities allow us to communicate complex and abstract ideas—like the ones you're reading now.

But just because we *can* do all of that doesn't mean we always make the best decisions. Why is that?

There are many reasons for this, and they are the subject of many books and a great deal of scholarship. But let's touch on a few points relevant to making future-ready decisions in our technology-driven world, with the aim of minimizing harm, risk, and regret.

To begin with, it's hard to care about things you can't picture. It's hard to visualize the difference between very large numbers, for example, or between orders of magnitude of large numbers. Try imagining the difference between millions, billions, and trillions. It's tough.

It's also difficult to picture exponential effects. Early in the COVID pandemic when the case counts in some areas were doubling every few days, but the overall number of cases was still low, it was deceptively easy for people to downplay the severity, at least in part because it's hard to grasp that 2 can become 2000 after just 10 doublings.

Take a fascinating study (which is sometimes cited in relation to the effective altruism movement). People were asked how much they'd pay to save migratory birds from drowning in oil ponds. For 2000 birds, they'd pay $80; for 20 000 birds, $78; and for 200 000 birds, $88 (Desvousges et al. 2010).

This is not rational, but it kind of makes sense, doesn't it? We're just not very good at visualizing large numbers or abstraction or being consistent with the value we place on either. This cognitive bias is known as scope insensitivity, and it relates to what the late Daniel Kahneman called our system 1 thinking: faster, intuitive, and often our go-to in a crunch (versus the slower, more deliberate, more analytical, and more effortful system 2). System 1 is quick! Great for escaping tigers, not so much for mathematical consistency.

When we're forced to think and act quickly, we lean heavily on instinctive thinking, but it's easily misled. In essence, our incredible brains can both elevate and hinder us.

As we navigate a world amplified by technology, recognizing and understanding mental shortcuts can lead us to wiser choices. Ever find yourself going numb? Wrestling with acting on what you know? That's related to our struggle to envision the future. We spot trouble ahead but stick to our old ways. Instead of changing, we stew in anxiety or hide behind denial.

That future reality often feels distant, abstract. Exponential growth? We're not really wired to grasp it. Our rationality plays by the pictures in our heads, not by the actual scale of things.

That's why understanding the impact of AI systems on all manner of human experience is tough. It's not just about scale; it's about our brains favoring immediate threats over complex, distant ones. Not the ones that require math. Or really any complexity.

But this is where technology can be a teammate. Algorithms and data can flag when things are off-kilter, such as a spike or weird patterns in some KPI (key performance indicator). Notify me when there's a greater than usual percentage growth in users, or when the usage metrics deviate in significant ways. In other words, smart alerts for the stuff that matters.

Our brains prefer familiar paths—call it commitment or call it consistency bias. But sticking to our core values doesn't mean we can't adapt details for a bigger impact.

There's a lot out there on cognitive biases; a few points are worth mentioning in relation to future-ready thinking and decision-making. First, our brains are wired for short-term thinking. This made sense from an evolutionary standpoint—survival depended on reacting quickly to immediate threats such as natural disasters or predators. Again, with the tigers. But in the too-fast world of tech, this can be a hindrance: these decisions can have long-term consequences. We often prioritize immediate gratification over long-term benefits, which can lead to poor decision-making in the face of complex and uncertain challenges.

Second, our brains also have a negativity bias, meaning we pay more attention to negative information than positive information. This too was useful from an evolutionary perspective: paying close attention to potential threats helped us survive in dangerous environments. (Tigers!) However, in today's world where we are bombarded with constant negative news and information, this bias can lead to feelings of anxiety and fear that may prevent us from thinking clearly and making sound decisions.

Finally, our brains tend to seek out confirmation of our existing beliefs rather than actively seeking out new information or perspectives. This confirmation bias can limit our ability to see the full picture and consider alternative viewpoints, hindering our ability to make well-informed decisions.

Thinking Language

When we talk about the human brain, we often fumble for language that seems suited to the complexity of the subject. Every generation tends to describe it using whatever is the most sophisticated technology of the moment: mechanistic, calculating, computing, etc.

But contrast this with microprocessors, and computing machines that are made for information processing and retrieval; we're not meant to solve retrieval problems. We're better off delegating that to machines and getting good at how we use machines to do that.

Human brains aren't mechanisms, they aren't calculators, and they certainly aren't computers. They are controllers of the human body. Specifically, they are for guiding the human body to survive and flourish in challenging environments by embodying learnings into connected ideas. They are meaning-making magic, specifically embodied meaning.

The Embodiment of Intelligence

Human intelligence is inextricably tied to our bodies; we process and understand the world through embodied sensory experiences. We make meaning through our senses. When we talk about things "making sense," that's part of what that refers to.

Humanity isn't alone in this—certainly nonhuman animals process embodied information, too. They sense their surroundings, they have intuitive defenses and instincts, and they remember and learn relative to the embodied experiences they have.

Artificial intelligence that runs in a box, however, may be able to synthesize a great deal of existing information and accumulated knowledge and even construct new ideas with it, but that isn't the same as making sense. Machines without bodies cannot make sense in the way we do.

Does that mean that AI models, lacking embodied experiences, are limited? Or does it mean that *we* are limited? It depends. This doesn't necessarily make one form of intelligence superior to the other. It simply means they are different, and these differences may be complementary. By understanding how to pair the advantages of human cognition with the strengths of AI, we can harness the potential of this powerful synergy.

For some applications, disembodied machine intelligence that provides fast calculations, pattern connections, and new ideas will have an advantage. And it will be to our advantage to use that capability. But for other applications, our human ability to make sense of the world and comprehend things in context, given emotional cues, instinct, and good judgment, will have the advantage. And it's going to be to our collective benefit to understand how to pair these advantages.

By doing this well and carefully, we pave the way for a future where humans and machines can work together seamlessly, enhancing each other's capabilities. This symbiosis can lead to unprecedented levels of innovation and efficiency, provided it is approached with caution and responsibility, ensuring that AI systems are not only powerful and intuitive but also fair, secure, and aligned with human values and ethics.

Applying the Strengths of Human and Machine Intelligence

As you make your way through this book, your brain is busily storing away memories as well as surfacing reminiscent examples for you to parse. Within your brain the hippocampus plays a big role in that formation, storage, and retrieval. In essence, it's aiding in memory recall and using your past experiences to inform your future decisions.

In 2019 researchers at DeepMind made a fascinating breakthrough: they created AI technology that "replays" stored experiences much like the hippocampus does in the human brain (Liu et al. 2019).

What shall we call this hybrid function, by the way? It's not "remembering," exactly. The language we use to describe AI can often be misleading. Ascribing terms like "seeing," "hearing," or "remembering" to AI risks anthropomorphizing machines prematurely. I'm as cautious of using language that suggests that AI has humanlike senses as I am about the term "hallucination" to describe a LLM misfire that results, fundamentally, in misinformation.

Regardless of what we call it, this achievement of AI in parallel with human cognition not only highlights the potential for artificial intelligence to emulate complex human cognitive functions but also underscores a common goal between human cognitive development and AI advancement: to optimize the process of learning from the past to improve future outcomes. **We want to use our past experiences to make better decisions.**

With the right tools and intellectual discipline, our cognitive processes can allow us to take a vast array of seemingly unrelated factors and weave them into a coherent decision. DeepMind's AI accomplishment showed some promise at bridging that gap by enabling machines to not only process vast amounts of data but also comprehend and interact with the complexity of our world in a way that mirrors human intuition. This achievement underscores a common goal between human cognitive development and AI advancement: to optimize the process of learning from the past to improve future outcomes.

What Humans Decide vs. What Machines Decide

Ever since our ancestors decided to come down from trees, making decisions has been part of the human evolutionary journey. We make thousands of choices every day, ranging from simple—such as choosing our breakfast—to those with far-reaching impact, such as selecting our life partners. Over time, we've gotten pretty good at all this choosing and deciding. It's a fascinating topic, how these processes happen in our brains. And it leads directly into questions of what we've learned in the field of machine intelligence about synthesizing decision-making—and whether it makes more sense for humans or machines to make particular decisions.

Where parallels exist between how humans and machines "think" and "decide" (scare quotes for the machine side of the equation, I suppose), they are there by design, but that makes them no less compelling. The similarities and differences between the approaches and the outcomes pose important questions about our future. As artificial intelligence grows ever more sophisticated, machines are encroaching on areas once believed to be uniquely human, but they're doing so alongside increasing human curiosity about just how far we can and should push the envelope.

Where vast amounts of data crunching are involved, such as in medical diagnosis, the power of machine processing is clear. Even a decade ago IBM's Watson was already capable of sifting through millions of pages of medical literature, diagnosing diseases, and suggesting treatments faster than any human doctor could (Friedman 2014). Today, with conversational interfaces to sophisticated AI models, patients can describe complicated symptoms to chatbots that don't run out of time or patience, and potentially diagnose issues on their own. And even though medical experts would advise tremendous caution, it has been known to work, such as when a mother was able to track down a rare diagnosis for her child's symptoms through ChatGPT (Garfinkle 2023).

We can't overlook the need for human validation in these scenarios, of course. The future of decision-making is not about surrendering all control to machines. But the legwork, the collaboration, if you will—finding the balance that leverages both human and machine strengths is the opportunity.

Both human and machine decision-making have their strengths and weaknesses. Machines, operating like superfast librarians, can process large amounts of data quickly. (Sort of. More on this later.) They can also make decisions based on predetermined rules or logic.

Outsourcing more decision-making to machines could lead to more efficient results and more precise outcomes. Machines can process data quickly and accurately, and while they are susceptible to the human biases they inherit from their training data, they are not subject to the whims of the variability and unpredictability that characterize human experience, including little things such as moods and hunger. On the other hand, humans excel at intuitive decisions, understanding context, and navigating the complexities of the real world.

The ideal decision-maker, be it human or machine, hinges on the situation. For example, in a high-stakes, time-sensitive context such as an emergency room, a machine, like Watson, could offer lifesaving speed and accuracy. Conversely, in a nuanced, emotionally charged situation such as conflict resolution, a human's empathy and understanding would be invaluable.

The more decisions we delegate to machines, the more control and flexibility around those outcomes we potentially forfeit, like setting a train on its tracks with no ability for it to deviate from its predetermined path. It could also mean a loss of visibility into why decisions are being made the way they are, and a loss of adaptability for shaping the future. Or it could mean more of all these things.

What do these strengths and trade-offs mean for our future and for the future of decision making? Will we hand over the reins to machines in our work environments, or delegate the driving to self-driving cars? How do we ensure the ethicality of algorithmic decisions that directly influence human experiences?

There are a lot of questions and not a lot of answers yet. Appropriately enough, it will all come down to the decisions we make.

Why Decisions Involving AI and Data Systems Are Complex

Though I loathe comparing technology to humans, it is tempting, in the current state of AI systems development, to compare it to a teenager who's suddenly hit a growth spurt. It's growing, changing, and evolving in ways we struggle to understand. It's trying to find its own way to solve problems, often choosing paths we, as human trainers, would never have thought to specify as nonsolutions. It can feel as though AI has its own mind, making decisions that are based on very large datasets, complex mathematics, and a tendency to take the path of least resistance.

The decisions AI systems make can be as baffling as they are impressive. It's a bit like watching a magician pull a rabbit out of a hat. We're astounded by the outcome but left scratching our heads as to how it happened. This is what we often refer to as the black box of AI.

Watching this unfold is both intoxicating and intimidating. An AI-driven world could offer limitless potential, but it clearly also presents unique and often unforeseen challenges.

This is the paradox of AI as a technology category: it's a powerful set of tools that can transform our businesses and societies, yet it's also a Pandora's box of ethical and practical implications. And its widespread adoption is driving the urgency for us to articulate our approach.

Technical Debt, Societal Technical Debt, Ethical Debt, Decision Debt

The concept of technical debt is well known in the tech industry, where taking shortcuts can lead to more extensive work in the future. But the less-talked-about ethical debt can have similar, if not more severe, repercussions. Ignoring ethics can lead to unforeseen issues and complications that affect the overall progress and reputation of the organization.

Google's Project Maven serves as a poignant example. The project is a collaboration with the Pentagon, aimed to develop AI that could interpret video images and improve drone strike accuracy. However, the project faced significant backlash from Google employees, 3000 of whom signed an internal petition asking CEO Sundar Pichai to cancel the project and enforce a policy against building warfare technology. They argued it violated Google's "Don't be evil" motto and could hurt its ability to attract talent (Gray 2018). The episode led to a very public discussion about the ethical implications of AI. Faced with the ethical debt, Google decided not to renew the contract, demonstrating how ethics can influence the course of innovation.

The concept of technical debt illustrates a similar short-term versus long-term dilemma, not only in coding practices but also in the broader societal challenges we face. It's like we're borrowing from our future selves, choosing the easy path now without thinking about the mess we will leave behind. And it's not just in coding. It's a metaphor for bigger problems we're facing as a society. All too frequently, we're making choices that are about the quick win, not thinking about the complex problems we're storing up for later, leading to what could be termed *societal technical debt*.

The crux of our challenge is, as we integrate technology into experiences, how can we ensure that they are meaningful at scale? Technology is the tool we rely on to bridge the gap between individual creativity and mass application. But as we harness these tools, we often find ourselves grappling with issues related to accessibility, user engagement, and personalization. How do we ensure that the solutions we develop are accessible to all, engaging on a personal level, and scalable across diverse audiences?

As we make data-driven decisions and encode these into our algorithms and AI models, we must guard against embedding shortsighted perspectives into our systems while simultaneously avoiding the extreme longtermist view that sacrifices today's human experience for a distant future humanity. It's paradoxical, as always, but we must strike a balance between the two. Either form of bias, once ingrained, becomes a legacy and a burden for future generations to carry.

This caution is underscored by the tendency to hyper-personalize content and experiences, illustrated by reports that Mark Zuckerberg once highlighted the immediate relevance of local events like "A squirrel dying in front of your house" over global tragedies (Kirkpatrick 2010), pointing to the complex debate over what we choose to pay attention to versus what we ought to find relevant.

The significance of this debate became especially clear throughout the mid- to late 2010s. Notably, in 2015 and 2016, Facebook's adjustments to its newsfeed algorithm had the net effect of prioritizing content from friends and family, and deprioritizing content from media outlets and brands. Framed as a move toward more relevant user experiences, these changes occurred during the lead-up to the 2016 US presidential election, raising questions about access to diverse news sources for the 68% of American adults who at least occasionally relied on social media for news (Shearer and Matsa 2018). Suddenly, what users got was more about family milestones than major headlines. It was supposed to make our experiences more relevant, but did it also narrow our worldview just when we needed it broadened?

The algorithmic adjustments also favored content that garnered the most engagement. One could certainly argue that's an obvious metric for a social platform, and they would naturally want to optimize for engagement. But combined with this function as a source of news for many users, the move raised practical and philosophical questions: Is Facebook merely a social platform, or does it act more like a news medium? And if the latter, does it need to follow and be regulated by the protocols of news media?

This shift also cracked open a door for more manipulative content to go viral. It's like laying out a welcome mat for those looking to game the system for their own ends. It meant that radical and foreign influences could gain disproportionate influence by gaming reactions and virality.

The Cambridge Analytica scandal serves as a stark example of the profound impact that data analysis and targeted content can have on public opinion and behavior. They weren't just guessing; they knew, using vast amounts of information—hundreds of thousands of data points. Cambridge Analytica was able to craft highly effective strategies to sway the opinions and voting behaviors of the public.

This operation was not limited to a single political campaign; it was employed by figures such as Ted Cruz and Donald Trump, as well as Brexit-supporting groups, though the full extent of its influence on the Brexit referendum remains uncertain.

It's complicated. But as we implement and scale up technology and consider how to make the best decisions in doing so, it's critical that we remind ourselves of how these dynamics interact.

In a process called transfer learning, we instruct AI models to take existing learnings and use them as the foundation for new ones. It's an expedient and cost-effective approach, but it also means that many decisions are already baked into the AI's underlying dataset and implicit assumptions and decisions. This creates a kind of *decision-making debt*, where AI systems make decisions based on previously encoded human decisions.

In essence, we are transferring the human decisions that often trained underlying models along with AI-led decisions that followed the path of least resistance. We may increasingly find ourselves making decisions informed by AI-informed absurdities, which has made decisions based on prior human biases—a fascinating echo chamber of human-AI interaction.

Ethical AI Requires Transparency and Explainability

For years, as AI systems development grew more sophisticated and attracted greater investment, ethicists and advocates for responsible technology agreed on two core principles: transparency and explainability. Yet, these traits are often elusive in the world of AI. Many AI models are like inscrutable black boxes, where the decision-making processes remain largely inaccessible to human understanding.

Broadly speaking, AI systems make decisions in one of two ways. The first is when the AI model trains itself, learning from its own mistakes and successes like a child learning to walk. The second is when humans determine a set of rule-based decisions that get encoded as business logic or datasets or training into the AI model.

From here, the decisions can get weird.

Once you train an AI model, it typically finds its own path to solve a given problem. This solution is very often the path of least resistance, and it may be one a human trainer would never have imagined specifying as a nonsolution. The mechanism by which the AI model "solves" the problem can be unexpected, even absurd. But here's the kicker: these are the decisions we *can* see. Many more are hidden within the so-called black box of AI, the magic-adjacent models we discussed earlier. These decisions, cloaked in enormous datasets and mathematical complexity, are even more mysterious. They often make little sense to human observers—or in the context of society at large.

With its mathematically minded success at finding the path of least resistance, AI systems have an uncanny knack for amplifying the impacts of decisions, for better or worse. For instance, an algorithm on a platform such as YouTube may be designed to optimize engagement, but in doing so, can inadvertently send users spiraling down rabbit holes of increasingly radical content. The overall effect can be to amplify systemic inequities and societal harms, exacerbating the echo chamber effect and contributing to the polarization of societies.

In any case, the challenge proceeding from AI-based decisions is in interpretation. For example, a mortgage company may program a set of evaluation criteria for an AI tool to use when considering loan requests. But unless the tool was developed with explainability in mind (and it should have been), if the tool recommends denying a loan, the company may have little recourse for evaluating what specific criteria triggered the denial. In some cases, data has been used for this type of purpose that can be associated with demographic information that may have bias associated with it and on which it is illegal to discriminate.

The Importance of Explainability in AI Innovation

When Apple launched the Apple Card in partnership with Goldman Sachs, the tech world buzzed with excitement. Marketed as a blend of cutting-edge technology and financial innovation, it promised to revolutionize personal finance. Yet the questions that arose after its launch raised the specter of gender bias and algorithmic discrimination—and made a case for explainability in AI models.

It began when tech entrepreneur David Heinemeier Hansson took to Twitter to express his dismay: despite filing joint tax returns and sharing finances, his Apple Card credit limit was 20 times higher than his wife's (Telford 2019). Apple cofounder Steve Wozniak echoed the sentiment, revealing a similar discrepancy with his wife's credit limit (Associated Press 2019).

These revelations hinted at a potentially systemic issue. The New York Department of Financial Services quickly launched an investigation, probing Goldman Sachs for possible gender discrimination (NY DFS 2021). The questions raised were about the very transparency and fairness of AI systems in financial services.

Goldman Sachs, on its part, denied any gender bias, insisting that credit decisions were based on creditworthiness alone. Yet, experts pointed out a more insidious problem: even if gender wasn't an explicit factor, algorithms could discriminate indirectly through proxy variables. Imagine an algorithm that takes shopping patterns or ownership of specific types of credit cards into account. If these variables correlate with gender, discrimination can occur without anyone ever intending it (Knight 2019).

This highlights why explainability is such a critical issue in AI models. If we don't understand how decisions are made, how can we ensure they are fair? This isn't just a technical challenge; it's a leadership one. Leaders must champion transparency, demanding that AI systems can be audited, understood, and improved.

Explainability Beyond Bias

Not all explainability problems are about bias; some are about poor change management. One of the most benign but frustrating forms of opacity has to do with crusty artifacts of outdated decisions as companies move to digitally transform operations. In advising with companies around transformation strategy, I've encountered numerous instances where some complexity hinged on the difficulty of dealing with one piece of data. When we look deeper and ask how the data is being used, very often it's not being used at all. It's a legacy artifact of some previous middle manager who always liked to collect this information about her projects in one department, and it was never meant to be universalized to all departments.

I can also recall a project where the company brought me on to advise as they were implementing a machine learning solution for optimizing supply chains. Initially, this investment in AI tools had seemed like a straightforward improvement. However, they soon discovered that the algorithm favored suppliers in certain regions, inadvertently sidelining smaller, local businesses. Rectifying this required a deep dive into the algorithm's workings and a commitment to ethical sourcing practices.

These personal brushes with opacity in tech have always left me pondering the balance between efficiency and transparency, and considering how easily we follow the promise of AI systems right into the pitfalls of unmanaged change. If we so unquestioningly gather the data we think we need and these systems can so easily misinterpret it, what other problems might we be introducing?

The Apple Card controversy also opened broader conversations about shared finances and the unique challenges women face in building credit history. For instance, many women manage household finances yet find themselves with lower credit limits or scores, reflecting broader societal biases. This incident brought to light the inherent biases in credit scoring models and underscored the risks and benefits of using AI models in credit decisions.

Ask the Hard Questions

The fallout from the Apple Card highlighted the importance of asking hard questions to prevent unanticipated outcomes. Are our AI systems truly transparent? Do they reinforce biases? How can we ensure they are fair and just?

Questions like these help us cultivate a mindset of curiosity and skepticism to drive us toward deeper understanding and better decisions. It's not enough to rely on the promise of objective outputs from AI models. This controversy reminds us that even with the best technologies, we must remain vigilant. Question more, dig deeper, and demand better.

AI, at its best, should serve humanity. Ensuring that our systems do not perpetuate existing inequalities requires a nuanced understanding of both technology and the human contexts it operates within.

Transparency in AI

Across a wide variety of applications, one of the ethical challenges we face with AI systems is transparency, or more accurately, a lack thereof. As AI models become more complex and sophisticated, it becomes increasingly difficult to understand how they arrive at their decisions.

As it happens, one of the difficulties in governing AI systems is that in many cases we can't see the decision processes. This is improving, but much of AI involves opaque calculations, and sometimes the only way we can make any sense is looking at output to see what the AI model has decided.

This lack of transparency has far-reaching implications. It can lead to unfair practices such as digital tracking, profiling, biased hiring practices, unfair lending practices, and biases in health care delivery, urban planning, and law enforcement.

Dehumanizing Implications

To understand the scale of this challenge, we must consider the widespread implications. The inherent bias of AI models, stemming from the human decisions encoded into them, can perpetuate systemic inequities and exacerbate societal harms. This dehumanizing effect of AI-led decisions and outcomes is evident across various sectors, from education to finance, health care to urban planning, and beyond.

Consider the opaque decision-making in predictive **policing**, where AI systems are used to forecast potential crime hotspots. The calculations and biases within these systems remain hidden, leading to potential injustices and societal harm.

In **education**, AI systems monitor student performance and behavior, often without clear explanation or transparency around the guidelines.

In the field of **human resources**, AI tools are increasingly used in the recruitment process, screening résumés, and conducting initial interviews. However, here again the lack of transparency in these systems can easily lead to biased hiring practices and discrimination against certain groups of candidates.

In **health care**, algorithms are used to predict patient outcomes and inform care decisions. Make no mistake: this could save lives! However, without sufficient transparency into these algorithms, they can inadvertently perpetuate biases and disparities in health care delivery. That can just as easily *cost* lives, not to mention quality of life.

In **finance**, AI models are being used to approve or deny loans and credit, sometimes with little explanation for the reasoning behind these decisions, as previously discussed.

Within **criminal justice**, AI tools are being used to help determine sentencing and parole decisions. But without the ability to understand how these decisions are being made, there is a risk of perpetuating biases and unfair practices within the judicial system.

AI and data systems inform decisions in **urban planning and development** around resource planning, traffic and congestion projects, and other development initiatives. Without transparency into how these are being prioritized, the outcomes can perpetuate socio-spatial segregation and reinforce existing inequalities in access to urban resources and services.

AI-driven **surveillance** systems are increasingly used in public spaces, workplaces, and homes. The decisions behind who gets watched, when, and why are often opaque, leading to potential privacy violations and abuses of power.

Across these fields and more, we've given AI tools and systems far-reaching influence. We've made it the behind-the-scenes observer and mediator, silently influencing decisions and shaping outcomes. Yet, the lack of transparency we've often allowed these systems to have can lead to unfair practices, discrimination, and the perpetuation of systemic biases.

No one wants any of that. But where do we take our complaints?

The Accountability Gap

When we delegate decisions to AI models, we may think we're doing the most responsible thing. We may believe the system to be capable of making more objective, unbiased decisions than humans could make. But as we've laid out here, the machine learning processes are already informed by our biases, and they've often added their own mathematical shortcuts on top of it—potentially exacerbating what-ever our original slant may have been.

To counter these risks, scholars, activists, and other experts have long advocated not only for greater transparency but also for accountability in AI-driven decisions. But how do you hold a faceless entity accountable? How do you ensure fairness and equity when you can't see the decision processes? It's a challenge that's growing increasingly complex as AI systems continue to evolve.

AI's Promise and Peril

The first time I used a voice assistant, it felt as if I had hired my own personal secretary. It was frustrating, though, when the assis-tant couldn't understand my commands. I would have to speak the syntax precisely, enunciate my words clearly, and after all that, then modify the results to what I had intended from the outset. In other words, not a very good secretary.

This wasn't even my first personal encounter with both the limi-tations and potential of AI technology. For years in my work I'd been exposed to a range of approaches to machine learning that prom-ised mind-blowing results yet often required a heavy dose of human intervention. And the realities can get a lot trickier than that.

This is the reality of AI as a category of technology. It has been around for decades, mostly in helpful but mundane ways: screening our emails for spam, serving ads, recommending music and mov-ies, and recognizing (mostly) our voice commands. It's no longer an emerging phenomenon—that is, if you look at it from a tech-centric focus. If you look at it from a human-experience-centric focus, we are only at the start of a significant learning curve ahead.

Only with the advent of generative AI—with conversational inter-faces, using "natural" human language, in back-and-forth turn-taking that feels uncannily familiar to us from everyday encounters with other humans—have a critical mass of people begun to interact with it. The experience for many has been both fascinating and unnerving. We can't help reacting to it as if it were another being somehow like us.

And we still have a lot of unpacking to do to determine if we are to be excited or afraid, or both. (Both/and is my default answer to everything, and it's not a bad starting place here.)

Like the joke about a well-intentioned genie who mishears your wishes, AI technology can be a mixed blessing. For all its potential to enhance our lives, it has for years been deployed in ways that make ethicists raise eyebrows. It has been deployed in highly sensitive environments, such as medicine and education, without rigorous enough testing. It has been used to make parole recommendations based on the sometimes-biased prior decisions of human parole officers, to identify and misidentify suspects in crime videos, and to optimize social media feed for maximum engagement by offering content that gets maximum outrage reactions and steering us to increasingly polarized content. Suffice to say, the influence AI systems have had has not always been benign—by which I mean both in amplifying our own biased decisions and in scaling its own form of absurdity.

Even the use of AI models in e-commerce has long been a game changer but rife with question marks. In the early 2010s at my previous experience optimization firm, [meta]marketer, we worked with many clients who wanted to improve their online stores using product recommendations. We were able to enhance customer experience measurably by using AI components to generate tailored recommendations. Mostly we could see satisfaction metrics rising in parallel to revenue, and that was rewarding. But while pushing data tracking to its limits and tweaking the algorithms so that they yielded the greatest revenue metrics, questions naturally surfaced—for us, at least—about data privacy and the responsible use of customer information.

Human-Centered AI along the Now-Next Continuum

The dual tendencies of AI systems, then, are not so much about the technology itself, but our approach to it. But in its rapid ascent into the mainstream of business and consumer adoption AI tools—especially generative AI tools—have become a flashpoint for futuristic scenarios.

What will help us is to balance the immediate realities with the future visions across the now-next continuum.

On the present side of the continuum, we have the existing realities of AI systems: the need to get data privacy right, use unbiased algorithms, develop meaningful measures, and implement ethical practices. On the distant side, we have the future vision of AI: leveraging it for societal good, while ensuring its long-term implications align with our humanistic values.

With AI systems, the harms of inaction are not so easy to discern from the harms of action. Both come with risks. If we remain inactive, hesitant to adopt AI, we risk falling behind and missing out on technological advancements that could drive our business forward—and solve human problems at scale. Some leaders have been cautious in adopting AI, but the potential harms to a company's longevity from not embracing AI could outweigh the risks to them of implementing it. For instance, in the context of health care, AI holds immense potential to enhance disease diagnosis and treatment. Yet, if we rush in and act without fully understanding the implications, we risk implementing technologies that could lead to unintended consequences, the scale of which is hard to comprehend because of the capacity of the technology involved.

The risk of misuse of patient data or incorrect diagnoses by AI systems is a serious concern—and that risk is borne by both patients and companies. Interpretability is one of the major ethical challenges with AI models. As they become more complex and sophisticated, it becomes harder to understand how they arrive at their decisions. This lack of transparency can lead to a host of bad outcomes: human harms, of course, but also mistrust of AI, which can hinder its adoption.

Transparency and accountability are both paramount then. We need clear communication about a wide range of decisions and outcomes—about data collection practices, for example.

Data Systems at Scale

We need to be very intentional with the data we model in our organizations today because it becomes the basis for the algorithms we create tomorrow. And the algorithms we set in place today—the rules we codify about our organization—will shape the machine learning models of tomorrow. In turn, these models will guide the unsupervised deep learning and reinforcement environments that will enable AI systems to thrive in the future.

In other words, we need to approach these decisions with intention and clarity, recognizing that we're all making decisions that will influence how AI models grow in their successive generations.

In essence, what we decide to put into a data model today creates no less than *society* tomorrow. This is not hyperbole. What we build, what we measure, what we say all matters: the metrics we establish, the data we collect, and the goals we optimize for are all contributing to the world we will live in tomorrow.

Putting Privacy in Perspective

In my earlier years in technology, the concept of privacy was more of an afterthought than a primary concern. The focus was on growth, expansion, and pushing the boundaries of what was possible. We were busy building the future! Potential consequences such as privacy concerns seemed distant, less urgent. But as I immersed myself further in a wider range of businesses, I witnessed firsthand the consequences of this oversight.

For example, I regularly see companies collecting far more data than they need, simply because they can. In our rush to innovate and provide personalized experiences, we often collect vast amounts of data. But just because we can collect data doesn't mean we should. Data minimization is an essential practice. Over time, collecting excessive data can open companies up to significant privacy concerns and, in some cases, serious data breaches—and places us in a position of responsibility if there are leaks or breaches. Each piece of data we collect is a potential liability, and we must carefully weigh the benefits against the risks.

However, this lens on privacy, where it primarily concerns risk and compliance, is too narrow. We find ourselves entangled in discussions about data protection laws, General Data Protection Regulation (GDPR) compliance, and potential legal penalties. While these are undeniably important, we need to broaden the discussion. We need to shift the dialogue around privacy to one that focuses on ethical, human-centric decision-making that aligns today's concerns with a responsible future.

So how can we approach privacy in a way that aligns with the "what matters next" philosophy? We can start by shaping our data strategy around the question: "What data will we need to make insightful decisions?"

Beyond the legal and compliance aspects, privacy is fundamentally about respect—respect for our users' personal boundaries and their right to control their personal information. This shift in perspective goes beyond just avoiding legal penalties or protecting our brand reputation. Our primary responsibility when it comes to privacy is to navigate the trade-off between offering innovative, personalized experiences and respecting the personal boundaries of our users. It's about building trust with our users, showing them that we value their privacy as much as they do.

Privacy is no longer a peripheral concern. It's a cornerstone of our digital lives, a topic that surfaces in every boardroom each time we discuss a new product or service. And rightfully so.

The world is increasingly realizing the impact of data collection and its influence, including on voting patterns. Countries worldwide are considering the impacts on their governments and their citizens of data aggregation, for example, through social app algorithms. This mirrors the data ownership movements that grew out of the late 2010s awareness of data monetization. Privacy has become a global movement, not only at the consumer level but also at the government level.

The conversation around privacy is more than just a compliance checklist. It's a reflection of our values as leaders and organizations. Especially given the amplification of algorithmic optimization and AI systems, the decisions we make about data today will directly affect our collective future, and we need to make these decisions with a clear understanding of the potential consequences.

Digital Twins and Deepfakes

Allow me to paint a picture. You're sitting in your office in Seoul, working on a project when a video call comes in. It's a colleague from across the globe, and they're speaking in perfect Korean. The catch? You've known this person for years, and they don't speak a word of Korean. The person you're talking to isn't your colleague at all, but their digital twin.

A digital twin is essentially a digital clone. It looks like you, talks like you, and can even mimic your behavior. Increasingly, these proxies are being incorporated into growing business models. On one hand, this adds a new level of personalization in the digital space. For instance, they can craft a customized video message to a potential client or translate a sales pitch into another language, making it seem as if you fluently speak, say, Korean or Turkish.

One example that gave me pause was a friend's experiments with an avatar platform where he recorded a message and shared it in Spanish—a language that he doesn't speak. The recording by the app was so detailed in its synthesis, it even managed to include a faint hint of his British accent through the Spanish "recording." Hearing that subtle detail added a layer of authenticity, making it highly believable—and quite uncanny.

On the surface, this technology seems beneficial. Just think about the potential! The need for international travel could be reduced, as these digital proxies can take our place in meetings across the globe. This not only saves time but also significantly reduces our carbon footprint.

But the same technology that creates these helpful digital twins is also used to create deepfakes—a technology that uses artificial intelligence to create hyperrealistic but completely synthetic media. This technology category has a downside like a cliff. Deepfakes pose a significant challenge to the credibility and reliability of media, threatening the pillars of digital literacy, citizenship, democracy, and access to reliable information.

The misuse of this technology can lead to alarming consequences, such as impersonating individuals without their consent, a blatant violation of privacy rights. Nonconsensual pornography deepfakes are another sinister application. Certainly, pornography was the early primary use case for deepfakes: a 2019 study found that 96% of deepfake videos online were nonconsensual pornography (Ajder et al. 2019). The applications have broadened out since then, but the risks of identity theft and fraud still loom large.

And that uncanniness I mentioned earlier? It raises a lot of questions. Questions about privacy and the right to control one's likeness. Questions about trust, credibility, and fairness. The nature of deepfakes as video content means that they can undermine trust. Research on deception indicates that exposure to misinformation can erode trust in media overall, even if viewers aren't entirely deceived. This effect contributes to the "liar's dividend," a term coined by law professors Bobby Chesney and Danielle Citron. As public awareness of deepfakes increases, deceitful public figures may find it easier to evade accountability for what they've actually said or done, because they can always blame deepfakes.

On a more relational level, the use of digital proxies in business prompts questions about entitlement and appropriateness. For example, sending a digital proxy to attend a meeting on your behalf may seem efficient, but what message does it convey about the value we place on direct human interaction and respect for each other's time?

The bigger question is, what is the intent behind their use? Are we using technology to serve humanity, or are we allowing our fascination with its development to dictate our future?

Deepfakes are a manifestation of AI's creative potential but also a troubling source of misinformation. The ability to synthesize such convincing content and experiences presents us with a profound dilemma.

What's our response to this deepfake dilemma? We're turning to AI itself.

Trusting AI to Know When AI Can't Be Trusted

Faced with the potential of deepfakes to distort reality, we must question how we can trust AI—and whether AI can trust itself. Interestingly, we're training AI to recognize and flag untrustworthy AI-produced content.

It's a fascinating endeavor but also a paradoxical one that brings us to an intriguing question: What happens to AI when it recognizes its own fallibility? When it sees its own limitations?

It's perhaps not exactly like asking a mischievous child to police their own behavior, but by asking AI to effectively police itself, we are essentially asking AI to recognize when it—or its siblings—can't be trusted. In doing so, we are stepping into a realm of self-awareness and introspection not typically associated with machine learning.

The Ethics of Personhood

For all the mainstream discourse about "robots taking jobs," it was still a surprise to me one day in 2019 to find a robot doing *my* job. An event for which I was to deliver the closing keynote had also "hired" Sophia, the robot created by Hong Kong–based company Hanson Robotics, to be its opening keynote speaker.

Not that it was *completely* out of left field: Sophia had by then been an ever-present fixture in the tech media for a few years. In 2017 the humanoid robot, which was styled to resemble Audrey Hepburn, had even been granted full citizenship and a passport in Saudi Arabia. While it may have been easy to dismiss that as a publicity stunt—it's never been quite clear what the action meant in practical or legal terms, except that, for example, unlike human women in Saudi, Sophia does not have to be accompanied by a man in public—the decision nonetheless raised thought-provoking questions about the essence of personhood and the implications for AI.

The issue of personhood for robots and other entities with synthetic intelligence brings us face-to-face with a quandary that has been confined for decades mainly to the realm of science fiction and the most hardcore of tech enthusiasts. Should a robot be classified as a citizen or indeed regarded as a person? And if the answer is no for now, what criteria might need to be met to determine when that answer may change? These questions have taken on a new urgency and are no longer purely hypothetical.

But the ramifications of personhood for synthetic intelligences are murky at best. Responsibility for any harm they may cause is a gray area. Is the robot, or its creator, accountable? Complicating matters further is the fact that corporations have personhood in most countries around the world. In the United States, the Dictionary Act includes corporations within the definition of the word "person." This allows corporations to enter contracts, sue and be sued, and own property.

The premise of corporate personhood rests on the notion that ultimately, the beneficiaries of corporate actions are human citizens. But it also has the potential to shield individuals from liability for corporate actions. If a self-driving car, for example, causes the death of a pedestrian, who is responsible? The car, its owners, its developers, or the owners of the company who designed it? By extension, the potential for AI personhood to shield corporate responsibility is a real possibility.

As the legal implications of these issues evolve, we can acknowledge that conferring personhood on synthetic intelligences doesn't necessarily imply that we believe them to be humanlike and truly equivalent beings. Sophia is, in cultural terms, not really a person.

In the case of corporate personhood, it is understood that this is a useful fiction for legal purposes. But it still means corporations have certain rights, such as privacy. This is very likely the model we'll borrow for AI.

Thinking ahead to the AI-powered experiences of the future, this raises significant concerns. In an ecosystem where the rights of individual citizens are offset by the rights of corporations and by rights granted to synthetic agents, humans could end up on the losing side. While there are cases where corporate rights protect human rights, such as preventing search and seizure of records that would compromise individuals' privacy, there are undoubtedly situations where the balance of power is skewed.

The potential for this imbalance to undermine democracy is real. In a scenario where the rights of machines and corporations outweigh those of individuals, the balance of power in a democratic society can be significantly disrupted. Democracy, at its core, is a system that upholds the will and rights of the people. However, if artificial entities are granted personhood, and therefore rights, they could potentially be manipulated by a few individuals or corporations with control over these entities. This manipulation could undermine the democratic process, as these entities could influence decisions and policies in favor of their controllers, thereby diluting the voice and vote of the individual citizen. It could lead to a (greater) concentration of power and wealth, creating an (even more) unequal society that goes against the principles of democracy. The ethics of personhood, whether it relates to AI or corporations, has the potential to undermine human personhood. Therefore, it is critical to approach the concept of personhood for synthetic intelligences with extreme caution and rigorous ethical considerations.

Whack-a-Mole Regulations

Just six months after the public debut of ChatGPT on November 30, 2022, OpenAI CEO Sam Altman spent much of the Spring of 2023 making the rounds of various government hearings, advocating for the implementation of specific regulations to restrict AI. Some commentators (including yours truly) suggested that he could be attempting "regulatory capture," in which a group tries to sway a regulatory body, intended to serve the public good, toward instead advancing the specific commercial or political interests of special-interest groups that dominate the industry or sector it is charged with overseeing.

When it comes to AI and the policies under consideration there's a growing sense of urgency that we need to transcend such instances of regulatory capture. Our goal must be to forge a more balanced and equitable system that safeguards public interest while simultaneously fostering innovation and competitive dynamics.

In fact, this is a common question in my workshops and keynotes: Aren't regulators always going to be playing catch-up with technology? It's asked as if to suggest that retrofitting protections around existing technology is futile. But regulators will invariably lag behind technological advancements. In most cases we could make little progress on coherent debate around regulating technologies few people had seen in action yet. Often, the full ramifications of technology are obscure, unpredictable, and only well understood (beyond responsible tech practitioners and consultants) once they've been rolled out at scale—at which stage regulatory intervention becomes critical.

Recall the discussion of probability from Chapter 2. If we apply a probability lens here, we can see that it ought to be possible to anticipate a small range of likely next steps, and where we see problematic misuses and abuses, such as child pornography, nonconsensual pornographic deepfakes of real people, or identity fraud. This preparation can help us better establish necessary guardrails.

Besides, it's not new or uncommon to have to go back and retroactively fit consumer protections and other legislation around innovations already in the market. It wouldn't make much sense the other way. This approach, rather than being preemptive, ensures that necessary adjustments are made responsibly.

As for whether regulations hamper innovation, they may. But if they mostly curb the adverse effects of innovations that disregard humans' welfare, then they serve a vital purpose. Despite being perceived as limitations, regulations can offer substantial benefits in two ways. First, they mitigate risks through the establishment of guidelines and standards, which helps prevent companies from potential costly mistakes. Second, regulations can relieve business leaders from the burden of ethical dilemmas, as regulations create an equitable competitive environment, where leaders don't have to worry about being at a competitive disadvantage against less scrupulous competitors.

All of that said, the global nature of modern business adds a layer of complexity to this issue. Businesses operating across borders face unique challenges due to varying regional regulations. While some argue that regulation stifles innovation, a primary concern should be preventing foreign entities from exploiting regulatory gaps to penetrate markets unlawfully—and potentially causing unmanaged harms. This factor must be carefully considered when advocating for or implementing new regulations.

Ahead of Regulations

Numerous companies have shown a "what matters next" approach when it comes to getting ahead of regulations, particularly around sustainability. Swedish furniture giant **IKEA** made a commitment to become climate positive by 2030, aiming to reduce more greenhouse gas emissions than they emit. This commitment not only helps IKEA to prepare for potential future environmental regulations but also resonates with the growing number of consumers who prefer to buy from businesses with strong environmental values.

Unilever developed a Sustainable Living Plan, which outlines a strategy to decouple their growth from their environmental footprint, while increasing their positive social impact. This strategy allows Unilever to address current societal and environmental challenges, while preparing for a future where sustainable practices are expected by consumers and potentially mandated by regulations.

These examples don't speak solely to climate change or carbon neutrality; they demonstrate just as much relevance to tech regulations. But these companies' pledges and efforts to align with them are a powerful demonstration of how organizations can balance their current demands with recognition of the impending future and the courage to embrace it, not as a threat, but as an opportunity for growth, innovation, and transformation.

The Climate Footprint of AI Systems

But while we're speaking of climate: our journey into the AI landscape has been thrilling, but ethical dilemmas are our frequent travel companions. An often overlooked companion is AI's substantial environmental footprint. Imagine the energy consumption of a city that never sleeps. That's a striking comparison for the servers constantly running AI models. Like an invisible exhaust pipe, the servers are contributing to our warming planet. According to researchers, training a single AI model can produce about 626 000 pounds of carbon dioxide, equivalent to around 300 round-trip flights between New York and San Francisco (Kanungo 2023). And remember: that's just the *training*; the usage of the tools has its own footprint, and it's sizable. Large language models such as ChatGPT are notably more server-intensive than search engines, which means the usage trend toward generative AI displacing search brings a heavier carbon footprint: asking ChatGPT for an answer for which you might otherwise search Google could consume 7–10 times more energy (Flanagan n.d.). It's not always the most talked-about consequence amid the AI hype, but it's one we can't afford to ignore. Our decisions must take this hidden cost into account. Just as we seek energy-efficient appliances to reduce our personal carbon footprints, we should strive for energy-efficient AI solutions.

By 2040, emissions from the tech industry are expected to reach 14% of all emissions globally (Nordgren 2022).

Done right, though, all this *could* mean opportunity, too: even though AI systems consume a lot of energy, AI modeling is also one of the best hopes for getting the most efficiency from renewable energy sources. One recent estimate suggests that AI systems already serve around 50 different types of uses within the energy ecosystem, from monitoring and maintaining the grid to load balancing and forecasting (Allsup and Weinstein 2023).

AI systems are like buildings that consume significant energy all throughout the day and night, adding to our planet's warming. But what if we could make them green buildings? Pathways exist to reduce this environmental impact, and they must be a factor in our strategic plans.

As we plan, our strategies must look toward sustainability. This means aiming for net zero emissions from data centers and demanding transparency along the supply chain.

As an interim next step, our AI systems could become more like hybrid cars, consuming less, and producing fewer emissions.

We need to factor this into our decision-making process with through-line thinking, seeking out energy-efficient solutions and advocating for sustainable practices in AI development. If AI systems are to be part of our strategy, the only way for that strategy to be future-ready is to wrap it in a sustainable approach.

Now What? Now-Next

The future of AI is a vast territory, full of promise and peril. Navigating its ethical landscape is no easy task. There is no way to make sense of all this without an integrated view. Our steps must be carefully chosen. Each one must be aligned with where it takes us in the future but carefully placed for how it affects the current moment.

That means the key to successfully making progress with so much risk at stake lies in embracing a responsible incrementalism. Instead of making a giant leap toward our future vision, we should take small, carefully monitored steps. This approach allows us to learn and adapt as we progress, helping us avoid potential pitfalls and steer toward a future that benefits us all.

We must approach the whole field of AI technology with curiosity, responsibility, and humility. We must remember that we are shaping our future not just with a tool or a technology, but with a powerful force of acceleration that amplifies both our own decisions and its own calculations. It's our responsibility to ensure that this future aligns with our human values, leveraging AI systems' potential while mitigating their risks.

What that means, in practice, is integrating the best of human cognition into machine intelligence so that it can mirror the best of us back. Likewise, by harnessing the power of AI to enhance memory recall, decision-making, and learning, we can create a future where machines work in harmony with human intuition and elevate our collective potential for innovation and growth.

The interdependency this suggests, though, assumes the ethical deployment of AI systems. Particularly when we're talking about those that draw upon human cognitive processes for inspiration, it becomes increasingly important to understand and integrate trustworthy processes, comprehensive data protection measures, and safeguards against potential biases.

We must equip governments to do what most of us agree that we entrust them to do: oversee on the public's behalf. But that assumes a level of informed participation from business and civil society, so it is also our responsibility to be part of this process where we can add value to the discussion.

We need to begin to conceive of measures of progress and measures of safety. When we think of measuring automotive safety, we think about road accidents and fatalities. How do seat belts and airbags help us? What are the circumstances in which they may be harmful, such as with infant car seats? When it comes to AI systems, how might we make informed decisions around actual experiences in measurable ways?

Allow me to say what I've alluded to more explicitly: algorithms are inherently biased due to the human decisions encoded into them. At any and every level they can perpetuate systemic inequities and exacerbate societal harms.

Our most responsible recourse is to build them with greater diversity and inclusion upfront, and with greater transparency and accountability downstream of their impacts.

The best-case outcome for the future vision of AI is alluring: unprecedented conveniences, cures for diseases, the potential to leverage it for societal good. From where we stand on the "now" side of the continuum, the present realities of AI systems remind us of what we need to do next to have the best chance of building that future and not the worse alternative: we need to ensure data privacy, use unbiased algorithms, and implement ethical practices around AI models, systems, and tools.

Our approach to AI needs a healthy balance of curiosity, responsibility, and humility. It cannot prioritize the future over the needs of people living today; nor can our actions ignore the good that could be done by systems that may help us solve our biggest problems, such as climate change, disease, and famine. May we use it not just as a tool for economic progress but also as a catalyst for creating a future that truly matters to us all.

A Call to Action for Human-Friendly Tech Leadership

Whether we're excited or afraid (or both), one thing is certain: AI systems are reshaping our world in profound ways. The true promise of AI systems lies not just in their technological capabilities but also in their potential to augment our human experience—and that's for better *and* for worse. But with that potential, we have the power not just to advance technology but also to advance humanity—*if* we do it right.

Decision Tool: Harms Consideration Checklist

Immediate user impact: How will this decision affect our immediate users? Are there potential negative consequences for their experience or well-being?

1. **Wider societal impact:** Beyond our immediate users, how might our decision ripple out into the wider society? Could there be unintended consequences that affect individuals or groups outside of our immediate user base?

2. **Environmental impact:** Does our decision have potential environmental consequences, whether through resource usage, waste, or other factors?

3. **Economic impact:** Consider the potential economic impacts, both for the organization and for the wider economy. Could this decision lead to job losses, or conversely, could it spur economic growth?

4. **Long-term impact:** What are the potential long-term consequences of this decision? How might it shape our organization, our users, and our society in the years to come?

5. **Harms of inaction:** What might be the consequences of not making this decision? Could there be harms associated with maintaining the status quo?

6. **Harms of action:** Contrastingly, what could be the negative consequences of taking this action? Could it lead to backlash, financial loss, or other negative outcomes?

Use this checklist as a starting point for discussions with your team. The goal is to anticipate potential harms and address them proactively in your decision-making process.

CHAPTER 5

Ethical Acceleration

Making Human-Friendly Tech Decisions Better and Faster

In first grade, I became a twofold state champion: one award for a computer game I developed named Doggie and the other for a book I wrote called *Herman the Horse Gets Lost*. Yes, I was an award-winning programmer, author, and avowed animal lover from a young age.

More importantly, these early achievements reveal computers and writing—or more broadly, technology and language—to be two of my lifelong fascinations, running side by side from the beginning. My 30-year journey in the tech industry has consistently circled back to these two passions, continually exploring how we *express human ideas and relationships through technology*.

That includes how we use technology to relate both to each other and to ourselves. And that's what this chapter is all about: making technology that, whatever else it does, stands ready to amplify the best of human experience—as well as the business practices that support that approach to technology for human thriving.

Harnessing Technology for Human Betterment

Can technology help us be better versions of ourselves? Can it enhance our relationships, make us better friends, partners, coworkers, and bosses? Consider the simple automated reminders that prevent us from forgetting a friend's birthday, or health data tracking that alerts us when something might be off. Gamified reminders can help us develop habits we want to cultivate, such as language learning and reading.

Technology can help us build better teams, communicate more effectively with our peers, meet our deadlines, and streamline our workflow. It can assist us when we're stuck. Can we also reimagine the current prompt relationship with conversational AI and have it prompt us when we're languishing—but only if it would be welcome, helpful, and not intrusive? What privacy would we need to ensure? What security? How responsibly would we need to be using data and caring for the users of our systems to ensure that we had their trust? These considerations and more are the ones we need to ask as we navigate our increasingly tech-driven world.

Tech that Uplifts Humanity

How do we create technology that amplifies our human characteristics? We start with a tool kit of fundamental human traits we'd like to uplift. Curiosity, creativity, empathy, and collaboration are essential, and they're capabilities that we can and should incorporate into our tech systems. Doing so intentionally, with an understanding of our role in the process, can lead to technology that truly serves us. Two more human fundamentals are meaning and language. Let's dig into them.

At the heart of every powerful insight and strategic decision lies a mystery we've been trying to solve for millennia: the quest for meaning. Meaning is *such* a fundamental human trait that I would argue it is the *most* fundamental. There's a lot to it. At its core, the search for meaning is about understanding. It's about finding patterns in the chaos of existence and making sense of them. Whether we find meaning through religion, philosophy, art, or simply by living our lives in the best way we can, the quest for understanding is a fundamental part of what it means to be human. It's about discovering our place in the universe and seeking truth in a world that is often confusing and unpredictable. It is also fundamentally about *what matters*. In a world where everything is ultimately temporary and nothing is guaranteed, what we choose to focus on and invest our time and energy in is what gives our lives meaning.

As we interact with the world around us, we continuously seek to understand how things fit together, how they work, how they affect us, and most importantly, *why they matter*. This is the process of making meaning, of meaning-making.

Meaning is a collective cultural construct that we use to interpret the world around us. We can discuss it at multiple levels, from semantics through patterns and purpose and truth, all the way out to the most macro questions of cosmic and existential understanding. At each level we can find different ways to look at the concept and how to interpret it. It's what allows us to communicate with each other, and it's also what allows us to understand the world around us.

In communication, you can think of meaning in three parts: what the speaker intended to convey, what was actually said, and what the listener understood. Where there is overlap between these elements, you have meaningfulness (see Fig. 5.1).

If you read my preface, you will not be surprised to find me making the claim that language matters. But it does, and in surprising ways both in business and tech: as a tool of strategic alignment and as a proxy for meaning and understanding.

Language as a Key to Meaning

Since November 30, 2022, we have been firmly in the ChatGPT era. As it happens, this AI era that has been characterized by so much excitement over a large language model is a perfect synthesis of my interests. As a linguist by education[1] and a technologist throughout my career, I realize I'm in a unique position to see the relationship of these disciplines with a certain clarity.

Language is, after all, the fundamental human technology, and meaning, if you'll pardon the comparison, is its operating system. Language is how we share knowledge.

---

[1] I was a German major in my undergrad, with a Russian and linguistics double-minor and a concentration in international studies, and my grad work is in linguistics and language acquisition. I'm also something of a language magpie: a polyglot who has studied more than 30 languages—although I only speak a few well enough to order the next round.

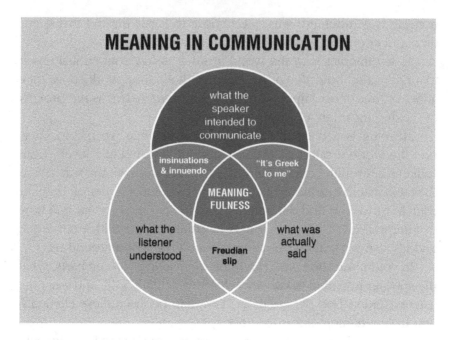

Figure 5.1 Meaning in communication.

It is also how we tell stories, make jokes, warn others of danger, and console those who are grieving. Language is also the principal means by which we construct our very sense of self. We use language to communicate our thoughts and feelings to others, as well as to think and feel about ourselves.

> "Language matters to us because it is a vehicle for meaning—it allows us to take the desires, intentions, and experiences in our heads and transmit a signal through space that makes those thoughts pop up in someone else's head."
> —Benjamin K. Bergen, *Louder Than Words* (Bergen 2012)

Meaning is what language does. All human beings are equipped with the hardware for meaning making: the capacity to produce and comprehend an infinite range of sounds and gestures, and to combine these into an infinite variety of sentences to communicate and create meaning. This capacity is what we share with other members of our species. It is also what we share with other animals that communicate: bees, chimpanzees, parrots—arguably *all* animals, and even plants. Without language, we would be limited to our own experiences and would have no way of understanding or communicating with others.

Language as a Tool of Strategic Purpose and Clarity

Meaning also takes shape in business as purpose. We're not talking about "purpose" as some abstract ideal or some out-there fluffy concept; we are talking about it as a disciplined central organizing strategic concept. It's about aligning people across diverse job functions to do useful work that contributes to the organization with the tools at their disposal. And by "tools" I don't mean just physical products or structures or systems; I mean the way we work together and the way we manage our businesses.

You get to this articulation of strategic purpose by distilling **what your organization is** and **why it exists** into a coherent idea, preferably no more than a few words long—aim for three to five words.

Because humans crave meaning, purpose is a fundamental concept in strategy—but that doesn't mean it's easy. It's tough to define and tough to use. But when alignment through purpose works, it creates a whole different way of seeing what you are doing, why you're doing it, and how much value it really has.

AI, Meaning, and Probability

Large language models such as ChatGPT and other assistants often seem to understand us, but have they really? Imagine you're planning a trip to, let's say, Germany and you'd like to prepare. There's most likely a set of English words including "airplane" and "road" that you'd like to learn in Deutsch: "Flugzeug" and "Strasse."

A computer model, such as Google Translate, can help you do that. That machine translation model would be, appropriately for our discussion here, a *transformer*.

Interestingly, LLMs such as ChatGPT are transformers too. They scan through a list of words and calculate the likelihood of any given word being next in the sequence. And it's doing this repeatedly. But here's the catch: The output from these models is not meaning, it's probability. It's a statistically calculated output most likely to be *interpreted* as meaningful.

To illustrate this, let's compare a Picasso painting with a Dall-E output that has Picasso-like qualities. The original Picasso artwork is human-created and is understood as being art, while the Dall-E output is something that merely has the *probability of being interpreted* as art.

The difference is even more stark when we consider a human therapist and a conversational AI therapy bot. One provides care as we understand it, while the other generates statistically calculated output most likely to be *probabilistically interpreted* as care.

That doesn't mean that those distinctions aren't likely to get blurrier and finer over time—as they should, if we want to create a world where most human experiences, many of which are automated, can be understood as meaningful, and not just as *uncannily almost like* a meaningful experience.

Language Is a Human Tool for Meaning

Of course, machines now also have language—multiple forms—and can communicate with us and with each other. But meaning is something that only human beings can do. Meaning is what we use language for. For us, language is the tool, and meaning is its product. For machines, math is the tool, and language is its product.

The capacity for making meaning is part of our human nature. It is not a cultural artifact that we learn from others; it is something innate. Language is an instinct, like the ability to walk or talk. For most of us, we don't have to be taught how to produce or comprehend language; we do it naturally, without effort.

This distinction in the way humans and machines use language is important because it is the basis for what distinguishes us—in terms of thinking, decision-making, and beyond.

The Role of Improbability in Meaning

In an ironic twist, improbability often adds to meaning. The more probable a sequence of words, the less information it contains. Think about it: if I am holding a cat, and I say, "this is a..." and my next word is "cat," that is a very probable next word, but it is generally not a very informative thing to say. It adds little meaning to your understanding of the whole feline situation. But if I say, "this is a. . . knife-clawed demon who enjoys nothing more than knocking glassware off the table," well, now we've got a story. The improbability of my words added meaning informed by sensory experience and observation. And with your own meaning-making brain you were likely able to visualize the glass shattering on the floor.

Again, probability is inversely related to information and meaning. As we work with large language models, their tendency is going to be probabilistic. We have to be the ones to keep bringing meaning back into the process, or otherwise we risk letting every experience become less meaningful as automation increases.

The Ongoing Importance of Meaning-Making

Despite the limitations of AI, we humans are the ultimate gatekeepers of meaning. Our expertise on what is meaningful is drawn from our understanding of the big-picture context of how a given passage or visual result fits into the world as we see and experience it—and as we sense and feel and think and reason about whether something has meaning.

We determine whether AI outputs are meaningful, both overtly and implicitly. If we don't like the output from a generative model, by *explicit determination*, we can rewrite the prompt. If we don't engage with algorithmically mediated recommendations that don't resonate with us, by *implied determination*, we send a signal that it's incorrect.

For instance, if we're presented with a recommendation in an e-commerce environment and we don't like the output, simply not clicking or buying it or engaging with it in any way sends a deterministic signal that it is incorrect. If enough people react the same way, that means someone else will eventually be revising the algorithm or the offerings will lead to a different outcome. Again, the point is: we're the ones deciding the meaning.

At the same time, we need to understand our own decision-making steps, as part of the "human learning algorithm" as well as how we learn alongside machines.

External vs. Internal Purpose

Machines, from the most rudimentary to the most sophisticated, are inherently devoid of purpose, except for the directives encoded into them during their creation and programming. They can be fine-tuned to perform tasks with precision, carrying out their programmed mandate to the letter. This is arguably a form of purpose, but it's an externally assigned one, a reflection of the purpose of their creators.

Humans, by contrast, are teeming with a sense of purpose, a product of our inner world, our consciousness. Our original evolutionary purpose may be simply survival and procreation, but our abstract awareness and interiority has deepened and dimensionalized that to a sense of the cosmic and infinite. We don't just carry out tasks; we question, we ponder, we connect abstract concepts, and we derive meaning through our experiences.

When we watch a sunset, it's not merely the observation of a celestial body sinking below the horizon. It's a symphony of colors painting the sky, a poignant reminder of the day that has passed, perhaps even a metaphor for endings and beginnings. It may evoke tears, and we may not even understand why. It is an experience rich with meaning, and this meaning is not something a machine can fully comprehend—at least not in the way we do.

David Eagleman, a renowned neuroscientist, puts it this way: "Everything you experience—every sight, sound, smell—rather than being a direct experience, is an electrochemical rendition in a dark theater" (Eagleman 2016). Our experiences are simulations in our brains, but these simulations are imbued with an inner richness, a depth that machines are currently incapable of replicating.

This is not to downplay the capabilities of machines. On the contrary, synthetic systems can mimic understanding and generate outputs that seem meaningful. Emphasis on "seem." Remember that machine learning outputs are grounded in probability, not in the subjective, nuanced understanding of meaning that we humans have. That's important when it comes to the details and the nuance. Everything is important when we're talking about scale. Tiny becomes mighty with scale.

In our pursuit of efficiency with strategies at the intersection of humanity and technology, we must not lose sight of the esoterically human. Experiences shine when they not only serve practical purposes but also resonate with our human sense of meaning.

Take the example of a tech company designing a digital fitness coach. They could optimize the AI to deliver the most efficient workout routines, but what if they also included an understanding of the user's personal fitness journey? What if the AI could motivate the user by reminding them of how far they've come, or by celebrating milestones with them? This added layer of purpose could make the user's interaction with the AI not just useful but also deeply rewarding and inspiring.

We Can't Leave Meaning up to Machines

One of the things I often say in my keynotes is this essential truth: **we cannot leave meaning up to machines to determine**. We can't outsource meaning. What do I mean by this? Well, let's consider the vast sum of human output—every novel ever published, every piece of art ever created, and every last episode of *Gray's Anatomy*. Synthetic intelligent agents can synthesize all this information. Yet there will still be a chasm between *how* these agents process that output versus how *we*, as humans, process it all. Our sense of what matters is intrinsically bound to our species-level experiences. We are shaped by our existence in the world, by our keen awareness of life's value, and by the gentle cosmic nudges we receive throughout our lives. This understanding can't be replicated by machines. Therefore, we must resist the temptation to allow our understanding of what is meaningful to be shaped by our fascination with machines. We need to be active architects of the future of humanity.

This doesn't mean that machines don't have a role to play. They can speed up work that doesn't suffer from a lack of human insight. But when work requires human insight, it should *have* human insight. Machines don't have insight, but they can provoke insights in us if we ask the right questions.

Output vs. Outcome

Finally, there's a useful distinction to make between *output* and *outcome*. The output speaks to the immediate result in a shorter cycle of decision-making and processing, while the outcome speaks to the result.

Working with generative AI tools reinforces this distinction. We may write a prompt and get an output that isn't at all what we had in mind. So maybe we rewrite the prompt; maybe we determine that generative AI isn't the tool for this task to produce the outcome we're ultimately looking for. This even applies to our own thinking: Don't like the output? Revisit the thinking behind the decision-making. Run the process again.

After all, it's not the outcome until it's what's in place. And even then, history is just a series of snapshots; we can always aim to change a future outcome.

Making Tech Human-Friendly

In this too-fast world with AI accelerating at an unprecedented pace and businesses growing to colossal sizes, the concept of the human scale is more relevant than ever.

If we want to make tech that is more human-friendly, we will need to get the human fundamentals right. These include things such as creativity, curiosity, and more. We'll look at some of the considerations for doing this well.

Creativity

One of the big anxious questions people often have about an AI-driven future is: Will human creativity matter? It's hard to imagine a future where it doesn't. Creativity is at the heart of human expression and the human experience. It's as important for our future as it's ever been in our past, so it's important that the technology solutions we develop foster and empower this in the people who use them. AI can offer us a big lift in supporting our creative output, and we should prioritize having it do just that.

But human creativity isn't just about *having* creative ideas; it's about addressing the underlying systems that may need revamping to support the new ideas we develop. That level of integrative creativity demands an environment where disruptive ideas can not only dare be spoken but can *flourish*, where they can challenge the status quo and ignite groundbreaking innovations. Boldness, curiosity, and initiative are all oxygen for radical new ideas. Yet creativity often faces a paradox; it's desired yet often rejected in professional settings due to its inherent uncertainty.

So the existential question for organizations is: How do we foster creativity within our teams, how do we encourage new ideas, and how do we embrace them when we're lucky enough to see them surface?

Creativity in Constraint

Paradoxically, creativity often thrives in constraint. When we're forced to work within certain limits, we're compelled to think differently, to approach problems from unique angles. And it's often within these tight spaces that we find the most innovative solutions.

I always encourage teams to think about their most constrained users—whether that's to do with logistical constraints, accessibility constraints, supply chain, whatever it may be—and ask: How do you uplift *that* user?

Take the kitchen tool company Oxo, for example. They started designing tools for people with arthritis and other mobility issues. By focusing on this constrained group of users, they found creative solutions to make their products more accessible. And in doing so, they discovered something unexpected: people without those issues often preferred their solutions as well.

Creative Blocks

One of the major blockers in imagining radical new ideas, particularly in technology, is our inherent bias toward familiarity. We often conceive new technologies within the context of what we already know. This "tyranny of the familiar" can limit our ability to envision truly transformative possibilities. Similarly, we can fall prey to "techno-chauvinism," the belief that technology is always the solution. This can blind us to more human-centric possibilities.

Although creativity is the lifeblood of innovation, it is stifled in many professional settings. A 2012 study by Mueller, Melwani, and Goncalo found that people could recognize more novel ideas but saw them as riskier. And when asked to choose ideas for implementation, they tended toward safe choices, even when reminded that creativity is important. In other words, even when we explicitly tell people we want their creativity, they're going to be battling their own impulses to stifle their own ideas (Mueller, Melwani, and Goncalo 2011).

Why? Well, it's risky. We've all had our creative ideas rejected; for some people that forms a lasting impression. And depending on culture, in some work environments, people are used to having to show up as their professional selves in some sort of cloak of impermeability, some sort of shield that keeps them from revealing too much of themselves or too much that's vulnerable and not fully formed. That sort of posturing and protection is death to creativity. Inhibition is a blocker.

This reveals the paradox that poses the biggest threat to business innovation: even when we make innovation a priority, even when we explicitly say we want new ideas, we have to overcome our tendency to recoil from the inherent risks of creativity.

That makes it crucially important for leaders to put their money where their mouths are: if innovation is a priority, it must be demonstrated in meaningful ways throughout the organization.

The Songwriting Approach

How do we foster wide-open creativity within our teams? It's a question I posed to my friend Cliff Goldmacher, a successful songwriter turned corporate trainer. Cliff conducts songwriting workshops in organizations to unlock team creativity, encouraging them to embrace their imaginative sides and break down barriers that might inhibit the free exchange of ideas.

It's about not just encouraging creative ideas but also creating an environment where they're welcomed. Too often, people have their creative ideas rejected—they're used to having to put up a professional front, a shield that keeps them from revealing their most innovative yet vulnerable thoughts. This is detrimental to creativity. It's our responsibility to break down these walls and encourage open, uninhibited idea-sharing.

The Boldness to Rethink

Embracing creativity and innovation isn't just about being bold with our ideas—it's about having the audacity to address the underlying systems that need reworking to support those ideas.

Consider the future possibility where we don't rely on work and jobs to support us. Is that something we want or should want? That may be open to debate. But the thought underlies a great deal of anxiety many people have about automation and AI. So even if the idea itself may seem far-fetched, if it is indeed even a remote possibility, we would need to start thinking about the supporting systems required—health care, education, and more—because the current systems, especially in the US, are inadequate for this change. We're a long way away from having the social infrastructure to support this shift. This is simple through-line thinking: the more transformation we would need to do to catch up with a change, the more we benefit by getting ahead of it. And it's as true in the context of your organization as it is in this larger example of societal transformation. Future readiness requires that we bring genuine curiosity and let ourselves entertain radical new ideas. Nothing should be off the table or forbidden from discussion. Closing our eyes to possibilities doesn't make those possibilities impossible.

Embracing creativity is a journey, one that requires us to challenge our own biases, to foster an environment that encourages idea-sharing, and to be bold enough to rethink our systems. But it's a journey worth embarking on.

Curiosity

As AI weaves its way into our daily lives and decision-making, it's natural to wonder what truly distinguishes us as humans. By now we know better than to expect one singular answer: partial, conflicting answers still offer clues to insights. And one of the more compelling partial answers is indeed one of our most inherent traits: curiosity.

It's this curiosity that allows us to think for ourselves, to question, to learn, and to grow. It's at least among the traits that truly make us human. And it's a strength and advantage in the AI world, if we use it well.

Empathy, ingenuity, and curiosity define us as humans. We instinctively synthesize ideas, juxtaposing information, connecting experiences, and discovering insights in unique ways. Our unconscious mind is a rich reservoir of creativity, and it generates ideas that AI can't emulate, at least in terms of being relatable to other humans.

Yet, the rapid advance of technology tempts us to outsource our thinking, stifling our inherent curiosity. We do well to resist doing this too completely. By harnessing our human-centric traits—and yes, thoughtfully using AI to enhance them—we can navigate the challenges of automation, making informed decisions that align with our values.

Outsourcing Thought

We're wired a bit for laziness. That hasn't been all bad: our evolutionary history has programmed us to conserve energy. But this instinct makes us hesitant to expend effort on ill-defined projects with payoffs that we can't be sure of (Burton 2022). That brings us back to the challenges of hesitation, as we've already discussed, but it also brings up another consideration: in the AI age, this tendency becomes problematic. We can't expect to outsource our best thinking to machines and get the most human-friendly results.

AI seems to offer a tempting solution to lighten our cognitive load, making choices for us based on algorithms and data analytics. However, just as managers too often are rashly tempted to outsource labor tasks to AI without fully considering the consequences, we can all fall into the trap of thoughtlessly outsourcing our thinking to AI. This approach can result in a glut of meaningless, AI-generated content and decisions littering our world. Ethical acceleration, though, requires us to be present, aware, involved, and curious.

Making human-friendly tech decisions requires that we guide our own thoughts. Generative AI and other synthetic systems can be powerful tools to accelerate suggestions and ideas, to brute-force our way through limitations and break through blocks, but then we need to view the results critically, asking ourselves whether they truly reflect what we mean to say, what we mean to put into the world. Just as we must not litter the web with thoughtless, AI-generated content, we must also not litter the world with thoughtless, AI-generated decisions. We need to retain an active, present, thinking role in the decision-making process—especially when, on the other end of the output, AI and other technologies are going to amplify the consequences.

Cycles of Influence

Consider the last time a machine influenced your beliefs or decisions. It probably wasn't that long ago. AI algorithms subtly shape our thinking patterns by serving us content based on perceived preferences and behaviors. It's a cyclical process where we train these intelligent systems and, in turn, they shape our preferences and decisions.

Take Amazon's Alexa, for instance. Say you purchase one, and you interact with it, training it to cater to your needs. In turn, it shapes your interaction, subtly influencing your choices. In effect, it is training you right back: to interact with it in specific ways, shaping your preferences and decisions. This AI-driven cycle continues ad infinitum, subtly shaping our thinking and behavior over time.

Yanis Varoufakis, former Greek finance minister and current professor of economics at the University of Athens, discusses this in his book *Technofeudalism: What Killed Capitalism*, as well as in an interview with me on *The Tech Humanist Show* (O'Neill 2024):

> "And because of the advice that it gives you on what to buy—books, music, clothes, whatever, you know, cars—that makes you naturally completely rational, you'd have to listen to it, to pay attention to what it says. And then that same piece of machinery sends it to you directly bypassing all markets. So when you go on to Amazon.com, and the algorithm that runs Alexa runs the Amazon warehouse, runs the website, matches up particular sellers of binoculars or electric bicycles or whatever it is that you're buying. It sells it to you directly. And that's not the market—that bypasses the market."

In other words, the AI systems running platforms such as Amazon directly match sellers to you based on your preferences. But not only does this AI interaction cycle bypass traditional market systems; it's also bypassing our curiosity.

Curiosity: The Antidote to AI Malaise

None of this is to say that AI is the enemy. On the contrary, AI can be a powerful tool for innovation, efficiency, and growth. But we mustn't let it dictate our actions and decisions. Instead, when we show up with our best human qualities—our ability to empathize, our experiential creativity, our contextual awareness—we stand to make better, more informed, more ethical decisions.

Cultivating a culture of curiosity and critical thinking is key. Curiosity pushes us to question, to explore, to innovate. It challenges us not just to accept the choices presented by AI systems but also to understand the *why* and the *how*. Curiosity pushes us to think like humans.

It's not about resisting AI, but about fostering curiosity and learning to effectively channel it in our interactions with AI.

Collaboration and Play

Our relationship with AI is complicated, but it's evolving. I don't necessarily like when people use the word "collaboration" here, since that sounds like an equal partnership, but it is indeed *something* more like that than typical tool use, at least as it relates to our experience of the process. We show up differently than we do with a human coworker or collaborator. We may try different things. We may be more willing to get weird and creative. AI is transforming our approach to problem-solving, enabling us to explore ideas from new angles and encouraging us to push the boundaries of our creativity.

Consider an instance where I was exploring the seemingly unrelated concepts of cats and architecture. I wrote an essay for my email newsletter that pulled these two disparate ideas together based on two excerpts from books I was reading. The gist was that we have a human tendency to project meaning onto everything we encounter. I was quite pleased with it: the process had been a playful exploration of my own mind's ability to form meaningful connections.

But then I got curious: Could I get AI to make this leap as well? I fed the two excerpts to the large language model Claude, and—well, well. Surprisingly, Claude went right there. The essay it produced addressed the same key idea: that humans project meaning onto the world around us. Was its tone as delightful as mine? Nay. Of course not. But was it readable, and usable? Yeah, it pretty much was.

That kind of experiment lends credence to the idea that AI can be asked to make random connections, and it may sometimes find clearly identifiable winning combos by some measure. Finding disparate connections between ideas is what we humans like to call "creativity." Yet, the question remains: Can AI learn to find its own meaning in these juxtapositions? In a way that we, as humans, would recognize as meaningful? Imagine the possibilities if AI could surprise us with insightful intersections of distinct ideas. It would then serve as a tool that accelerates the process of generating random insights.

In the early days of ChatGPT, people shared online about the tests they had made of its capabilities with silly poetry, and other less silly demonstrations such as résumé-writing—some of which were trivial, but still potentially transformative. By now, though, there are increasingly sophisticated uses and case studies for purposes that go beyond fact-finding and content generation.

Some are using the conversational capabilities of LLMs as sounding boards for brainstorming businesses. Others are looking for a cowriting partner for books, movies, and more.

Of course, as we continue to interact with AI in these varied capacities, it behooves us to remember that the data we generate by interacting with these systems is being collected by the company that owns the model. That makes it all considerably less cute, but still: there's a lot of potential here.

Designing for the Human Scale

Every decision we make has human consequences. We must think about how we can design experiences that are not only efficient and scalable but also humanistic and ethical. In an ever-accelerating tech world, our job is not just to make decisions but also to shape the future in a way that prioritizes humanity.

As we find ourselves in an era of rapid technological advancement, with AI accelerating at an unprecedented pace and businesses growing to colossal sizes, the concept of the human scale is more crucial than ever.

Balancing Automation and Empathy

When we talk about automating certain processes, we're usually referring to the typical use cases. For instance, automating routine tasks such as password changes and account access can save us, and the users, a lot of hassle. However, people are not averages. We all have unique needs that may not fit neatly into the "typical" category.

In almost every industry, almost every time, we encounter edge cases we can't automate. Herein lies the need for empathetic exception handling. We need to build systems that can handle these exceptions with care and understanding.

Even when we automate commonly recurring needs, we can do so with empathy and an understanding of meaning and nuance. How do people want to get from A to B? How can we create a sense of brand voice? How can we encode our values? How can we ensure people experience a sense of trust? All these considerations matter significantly in delivering a successful user experience.

Automation beyond Efficiency

The concept of automation is not new. It's woven into our daily routines, from brewing morning coffee to executing intricate business processes. It streamlines our routines, enhances our productivity, and, quite literally, does the heavy lifting for us. For years now, automated systems have been driving a great deal of experiences.

As we continue to automate more of our lives, though, we must ask: Are we simply automating mundanity for efficiency? Couldn't we also be infusing meaning into these automated experiences?

There's a quote often attributed to Bill Gates, though its origins remain uncertain:

> "The first rule of any technology used in a business is that automation applied to an efficient operation will magnify the efficiency. The second rule is that automation applied to an inefficient operation will magnify the inefficiency."

This statement, though potent, only illuminates one facet of the story. While automation certainly boosts efficiency, are we automating the right things? Are we merely making the mundane more efficient, or are we considering how to include meaning in those automated processes? Could we even, through careful design, magnify that which is meaningful all around us?

Imagine a world where all our interactions and daily routines are automated, but they're all devoid of personality or sparkle, empathy, or context—a world filled with efficient but hollow experiences. If all we automate are the operations, we select for their likelihood to be meaningless, rote, mundane, routine, and dull, then that's all we'll have in the world around us. That's a world we must strive to avoid.

As we harness the power of automation and exponential technologies, we must ensure we're directing these powerful tools toward enhancing meaningful experiences as well, not just mitigating the mundane ones. **We need to see both the experiences automation creates *and* the experiences automation displaces.**

While it's logical to automate tedious tasks, we must also be conscious of the potential scale of automation. As more and more of our everyday experiences become automated, it's critical we ensure these experiences have some degree of what resonates with us as significant, relevant, contextual, and affirming.

The New First Rule of Technology

So, let's transform the quote to suit our current discussion:

> "The first rule of any technology used in a business is that automation applied to a *meaningful experience* will magnify the *meaning*. The second is that automation applied to an *absurd experience* will magnify the *absurdity*."

Our approach to automation must be well-rounded, striving for both relief from mundanity and amplification of meaningfulness. Even in the most futuristic scenarios where humans don't need work, where productivity proceeds with little human involvement, where humans obtain their income or means for survival from non-labor sources, we will still be surrounded by the experiences we create—and they're likely to be automated. Wouldn't we want them to be *good?*

Let's take this idea a step further. What if, instead of just focusing on identifying mundane tasks and automating them, we develop a habit of encoding our most meaningful understanding into what we automate?

Consider the possibilities of experiencing automated but meaningful interactions daily. As we progress toward a future where more and more of our everyday experiences and interactions are automated, it becomes even more crucial that these experiences are meaningful.

Consider further: If human work *were* to become obsolete, where would humans find the same sense of meaning that has historically been derived from work?

Here's something Bill Gates *did* write:

"It is true that as artificial intelligence gets more powerful, we need to ensure that it serves humanity and not the other way around. But this is an engineering problem. . . I am more interested in what you might call the purpose problem. . . if we solved big problems like hunger and disease, and the world kept getting more peaceful: What purpose would humans have then? What challenges would we be inspired to solve?"

Here you'll find some overlap in our thinking.

When we take that lens of meaning, and we look at what that implies for us, what it really suggests is that what we need to be doing is thinking about how to create purposeful, intentional, meaningful human experiences well designed at scale, using data and technology to scale the meaning of those experiences, the intention, the clarity of purpose in those experiences, because the capacity and scale of emerging technology is going to create outsized consequences.

Universal Basic Meaning

This brings us to an admittedly ambitious idea: universal basic meaning. This concept goes beyond the financial implications of job displacement due to automation, which often leads to discussions about universal basic income. We must also consider the nonfinancial resources of meaning and identity that work provides.

Because the truth is, the interconnectedness of data, algorithms, and emerging technologies is more and more a part of our everyday environments. They can create experiences that have an outsized impact on who we are and how we live our lives. It's important that we comprehend the way these systems change us.

As automation continues to evolve, the nature of work is undoubtedly changing. The implications of this shift on financial welfare and the overall economy are often discussed. After all, if you scratch the surface of any debate about automation and the future of work, you'll find there is an argument for universal basic income.

And certainly, from a purely survivalist standpoint that's an important consideration. But we also need to think beyond this consideration of the future of work.

We need to know what it is going to look like for people not to have the financial resources from working. We also need to understand how this model might concentrate power and opportunity into fewer and fewer hands.

Universal basic meaning is not meant to be a substitute for work or for meaningful employment. Instead, it's a vision for a future where meaningful experiences permeate our lives, regardless of whether they are related to our jobs or not. It's a radical idea, but one that demands our attention.

Humans derive a great deal of our personal identity and meaning from work. What we do is who we are. Our jobs—or our ancestors' jobs—in so many cases become our identities, as the long tradition of names, last names and family names, derived from professions demonstrates. Carpenter, Baker, Butcher, and so many others—and this happens across languages, not just English. Throughout the world and throughout human history, so much of who we are and what we are about comes from what we do for a living and what our ancestors have done for a living.

As I wrote in *Tech Humanist*:

We derive a tremendous amount of meaning from our work—the sense of accomplishment, of problems solved, of having provided for ourselves and for our families, of having contributed, of having value and self-worth.

. . . We must recognize the possibility of a post-human-work world, or at least a world where human work has fundamentally changed—so that as we look at automation, we see the impact on both the experiences automation creates and the experiences automation displaces. Because in the future scenario where all the human work has vanished, where do humans get the same sense of meaning? That meaning we have historically derived from work will have to come from something other than work. We need a better answer.

The concept of universal basic meaning is about using the power of automation to enhance our lives with meaningful experiences, not just efficient ones.

This takes us right back around to this idea that we should "automate with meaning." It is important that we now, in the early stages of automating human experiences, encode them with all the enlightenment, all the equity, all the evolved thinking we can.

The future of automation is not just about efficiency—it has to be about meaning, too. As we build the future, let's ensure we're not just automating the mundane. Let's commit to infusing our automated experiences with meaning, building a world that is not only more efficient but also more meaningful.

The Purposeful Role of Business Leadership

The equation is not just humanity and technology. It's humanity and technology, which was made by humans, operating in a system that was made by humans. Moreover, it's humans operating in a system that was made by humans but which is now amplified and accelerated by technology.

This is why when we talk about purpose as a tool in business and to design more human-centric technology, it's about aligning the meaningful contributions and understanding of all the people who are part of the process inside and outside the organization because purpose is the shape meaning takes in business.

Even at this high level of business strategy, language matters. The words you choose to represent the strategic organizational purpose of your business should be selected with care and intent.

Consider what happened when Google's parent company, Alphabet, took shape and they restructured documents such as the code of conduct. They weakened the clarity of the message with wording such as: "Employees of Alphabet and its subsidiaries and controlled affiliates should do the right thing—follow the law, act honorably, and treat co-workers with courtesy, support, and respect." Not that those principles aren't commendable; it's just that their former motto: "Don't be evil" was a whole lot more direct—and far more memorable (Alphabet 2024).

Future Visioning

When you think of Amsterdam, perhaps you imagine walking through the picturesque canals, the charming waterways that symbolize the city's resilience and ingenuity. They're part of the charm of the city. They're also part of an extensive system of dams and defensive water management to keep the city from being overwhelmed by the sea. The city of Amsterdam started out as a fishing village in the thirteenth century, at an elevation slightly above sea level. Over centuries, Amsterdam grew, expanding into lower-lying areas. Today, much of Amsterdam is below sea level. So you can imagine how rising ocean levels will only make future-planning more complicated for Amsterdam. That's the obvious problem. But Amsterdam's leaders weren't content with only dealing with the obvious. They dared to look further.

A few years back, I received a call from a leader within the city of Amsterdam. The conversation wasn't about the looming challenge of rising sea levels, but about the future of the city in the face of emerging technologies such as AI. They were contemplating the implications of a fight for tech talent, the transformation of city services, and how these would affect citizens' experience and their approach to city planning.

Even in the face of immediate challenges, leaders need to cast a bold vision for their organization's future. Amsterdam's leaders understood this. They had the foresight to consider how emerging technologies would shape their city's future.

Future visioning is not just about being bold. It's about asking meaningful questions that open avenues for future-readiness.

Amsterdam's leaders knew that the questions they asked were as important as the answers they sought; more than that, the questions they asked had the potential to *shape* the answers they *would* seek. Instead of framing their future visioning as a battle for survival, they chose to view it as setting the standard for future-readiness.

From Amsterdam to Your Organization

The Amsterdam leaders didn't just ask questions; they invited dialogue. They brought together business, education, and civic leaders from around the city and region to discuss the metropolis of the future. The head of a start-up accelerator program sat next to the dean of a university, and on the other side was a representative of the planning board for the whole region, with about a dozen other participants of similar relevance. Leaders shared ideas, found common ground, and identified opportunities for collaboration. Quite quickly partnership opportunities emerged around what might have been logistical barriers, such as ownership and governance of programs that would span multiple entities.

The collaborative element of the Amsterdam story was pivotal. It transformed talk into action. It's a lesson that can be applied across all organizations. Whether you're leading a corporation or a city, the principles remain the same.

Today Amsterdam is considered one of the most forward-thinking cities on this planet. The way they've adopted integrated technology in the citizen experience suits them perfectly. They're more future-ready than ever.

Tech Humanist Leadership for Ethical Acceleration

Let's look again at the meaningfulness model Venn diagram, only this time let's explore the relationship between business objectives, human outcomes, and technological capabilities. Where we have overlap, we have meaningfulness. That intersection is where the Tech Humanist leader focuses. This is where ethical acceleration is possible (see Fig. 5.2).

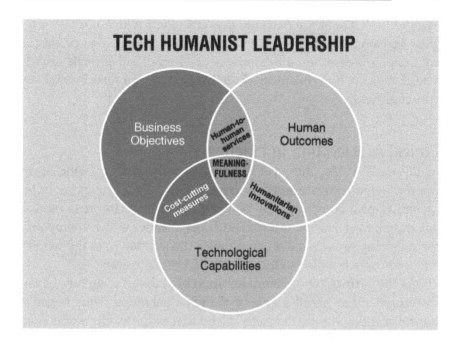

Figure 5.2   Tech Humanist leadership.

The Path to Purpose-Driven Growth

So what does it mean to achieve meaningful and sustainable growth? It involves aligning growth strategies with the core purpose and principles of your company.

Patagonia, of course, is a classic example. Their mission statement isn't about being the biggest outdoor apparel company; it's about building the best product, reducing impact, and using business to protect nature. Their commitment to their mission is so strong that on Black Friday 2011, they famously ran an ad in the *New York Times* stating, "Don't Buy This Jacket" to highlight the environmental cost of consumerism. The campaign resonated with their customers and strengthened their brand identity. Their growth proves that you can be both meaningful and profitable when your actions resonate with your customers' values.

A less obvious example is Warby Parker, an online eyewear retailer. Warby Parker's mission is to offer designer eyewear at a revolutionary price, while leading the way for socially conscious businesses.

They've built a platform that connects customers with affordable eye-wear and a unique home try-on experience. For every pair of glasses sold, a pair is distributed to someone in need. Their growth story is a testament to how business objectives can harmonize with social consciousness.

Ethical Acceleration in Practice

In the early 1970s, the world's energy needs were growing at an unprecedented rate. Amid this backdrop, DONG Energy, a state-owned Danish company, was building coal-fired plants and oil and gas rigs all over Europe (Morris 2018). As a leader in the energy sector, the company was making a significant contribution to the world's energy supply but also to the world's carbon emissions.

As the turn of the millennium approached, the company began to recognize the harmful effects of their operations. Thus began a transformation journey that would lead to a radical shift in direction, a rebranding, and a commitment to a more sustainable future.

By 2017, the company had committed to its transformation so fully that it renamed itself Ørsted, after Hans Christian Ørsted, the Danish physicist who discovered electromagnetism. The name change signaled more than a cosmetic alteration; it represented an ambitious pivot from fossil fuels to renewable energy. This bold move was met with skepticism by many, but Ørsted was firm in its conviction. Today, Ørsted is one of the world's leading producers of wind energy.

Ørsted's transformation wasn't just about changing the type of energy they produced; it was about catching up to their values. It took changing the company's entire identity to bring their purpose into alignment. In essence, Ørsted seemed to be proclaiming, "We are no longer DONG Energy, a company that produces fossil fuels. We are now Ørsted, a company that harnesses the power of wind for a more sustainable future."

The transformation from fossil fuels to renewable energy was a monumental decision, but it was just one of the many decisions Ørsted had to make along their journey. They became the first energy company in the world to transition from fossil fuels to clean energy. We can learn a lot from how Ørsted navigated these decisions.

Navigating Setbacks

Despite these achievements, Ørsted's journey hasn't been without challenges. Convincing critics—including shareholders—to embrace renewable energy as a profitable venture was tough. But they pushed through, sold fossil fuel businesses, won contracts to develop offshore wind farms in Germany and the UK, and made existing energy sites and construction more cost-effective.

One striking detail in Ørsted's journey is their commitment to maintain an ethical and human-centric approach amid external forces and crises. In 2022, amid the backdrop of the Russian war in Ukraine and the disruption of European energy markets, the Danish government ordered Ørsted to continue and resume operations of three of its power station units that run on coal and oil (Ørsted 2022). Ørsted complied, publicly stating that it recognizes its position to help alleviate the European energy crisis, but that society must phase out the use of fossil fuels as soon as possible. This decision was a powerful demonstration of their commitment to the well-being of all stakeholders and a strong example of navigating in real time the harms of action and harms of inaction.

Growth without Purpose

In business, growth is often mistaken for progress. But without purpose it's easy to fall into the trap of "growth at all costs." Take the cautionary tale of WeWork. In its rush to expand its offering of shared workspaces, the company invested heavily in new real estate properties. That led to rapid customer growth, but the costs of maintaining so many properties and services outpaced income, and the company couldn't turn a profit. This absence of a sustainable business model led to a significant decrease in its valuation and an uncertain future.

Responsibility requires that we also make risk-benefit decisions in line with purpose: mitigating risks and maximizing benefits while staying true to our ethical commitments. When Uber decided to test self-driving cars, a thorough risk-benefit analysis would have prompted more rigorous testing protocols, potentially preventing the tragic accident that occurred in 2018. As it was, the safety relied on a backup driver who was streaming a show on her phone and not watching the road ahead. While it is widely believed that

autonomous vehicles may ultimately lead to fewer accidents com-
pared with human drivers, testing them out on public roads requires
tremendous planning and care. A purposeful approach must ensure
growth is done responsibly.

Neither purpose nor responsibility guarantee profit and growth,
but growth without purpose or responsibility can more easily lead
to a vicious cycle of unsustainable practices. And sustainability,
despite our tendency to conflate it with environmentalism, is very
much aligned with profit. You can't sustain a business model that
doesn't pay for itself. Purpose, sustainability, and profit go hand in
hand in hand.

Purpose, Principles, and Profit

In the digital era, the balance we often need to strike is not only
between principles and profits but also in aligning customer goals
with business objectives—and this needs to happen before we use
technology to amplify and scale growth-seeking effects.

Some companies make the mistake of believing they can buy their
way to growth. They throw money at customer acquisition without
considering whether those customers align with their values or will
even stick around. This approach often results in wasted resources
and squandered customer goodwill. True growth is anchored in
the creation of meaningful customer relationships based on a deep
understanding of their needs and desires.

You can buy your way to growth but not meaning.
You can grow your way to scale but not purpose.

So what does it mean to achieve growth in a meaningful way?
It's about more than simply increasing your bottom line. It's about
understanding your customer's goals and how your business goals
align with theirs. Relevance is a form of respect. When you establish relationships with customers based on a deep understanding of
what motivates them, what drives them, and what language speaks
to them, you set the stage for growth that truly adds value. These
customer relationships flourish when customers believe that you are
solving their problems.

Indeed, a crucial piece of the puzzle is to align your data model
and technology to enable you to observe patterns and learn about

your customers, and to create a rich model of meaningful human experiences. This approach requires respect for your customers and a deep understanding of their motivations. Only with all these pieces in harmony can you offer efficiencies that work on both sides of the interaction, clarify priorities internally, and put resources where they matter most.

Consider Etsy, an online marketplace for handmade and vintage items. Etsy's mission is to keep commerce human, and they've built a platform that connects artisans with customers who value unique handmade items. By understanding their customers' motivations and desires, Etsy created a meaningful experience for both buyers and sellers, proving that growth can be aligned with the company's core purpose and principles.

Keeping principles in focus while adapting to changing circumstances is an ongoing challenge, however. Starbucks, for instance, has made claims to "100% ethical" sourcing, but lawsuits have alleged otherwise, claiming that the company sources from suppliers with "documented, severe human rights and labor abuses, including the use of child labor and forced labor" (Kavilanz 2024). The company continues to develop its own sourcing methodology, known as Coffee and Farmer Equity (C.A.F.E.) Practices, maintaining that it takes its standards seriously (Starbucks Corp. 2021). For many companies, the operational execution of principles—especially at global scale—is bound to be a work in progress. Yet we must commit to these principles with integrity.

Growth in a tech-accelerated context can be perilous if it's ill-considered, not suited to scale, and potentially detrimental to society, the planet, and so forth. Growth isn't inherently good, but if it's the mandate you've been given, what are you to do? In our quest for growth, we must not only aim to enhance the bottom line but also to enrich the lives of our customers and the world around us.

Learning to See Tomorrow

In my early days at Netflix, as one of the first 100 employees and the inaugural content manager, I was entrusted with the reins of the content database. It was packed with movie listings and their associated metadata—run time, rating, cast, etc. It was a world I was eager to dive into. But I quickly discovered a glaring flaw: each movie could only be classified under one genre. Imagine having to label the movie *Bridesmaids* as *just* a comedy with no added qualifiers, or *Oceans 11* as *only* an adventure and not as, say, a buddy comedy or even better: heist! So much wasted nuance—and more importantly, it was easy to see that down the road it would be too frustrating an experience for customers trying to find movies to watch. It was a limitation I knew we couldn't ignore.

This "genre project" became my mission. I led a monumental year-long endeavor that involved nearly everyone in the company. We reconstructed the database and reclassified every single film. Movies could now straddle multiple genres, and we even conjured up new conceptual categories.

What Matters/What Is Likely to Matter: Future-Readiness through Agility

Of course, the one-genre limit wasn't exactly a pressing problem at that time. The one-genre limit wasn't holding us back—yet. It wasn't what mattered at that moment. What mattered the most was outpacing Blockbuster and securing our place in the open market. But it was clearly something that was **likely to** matter down the road. It was easy to envision a dozen ways we might run into constraints in the future by not addressing that limitation now. Having the foresight to address a nonurgent issue that would matter in the future was a crucial step toward becoming future-ready.

Decision Tool: What's Your "Gift for Tomorrow" Project?

In sharing this story with audiences and clients over the years, I have learned three things:

First, **every company has a project like this**. A flaw. A bug. Technical debt. It's that sore tooth you know you need to fix.

Second, **data isn't just background noise; it shapes customer experiences**. It's the structure behind the scenes. Your data should reflect the customer experience like a mirror.

Third, it's about **future-readiness**. Fast-forward 20 years, and thanks to this project, Netflix now uses AI for pattern recognition, creating categories that wouldn't have been possible without address-ing our "genre project."

What's your "genre project?" What's the nonurgent issue you've been sidelining that could make a significant difference in the future?

You may find that some of the projects you've been putting off become easier to understand when you realize you're holding back what will matter tomorrow by not addressing it now because it doesn't seem like it matters today.

It's time to stop holding back what will matter tomorrow just because it doesn't seem like it matters today. It's time to ensure your business isn't just surviving today's market but is well prepared for the future.

In the end, it's not about moving fast—it's about moving thought-fully, with an eye on the horizon. We need to navigate the com-plexities of tech acceleration effectively, making progress by taking meaningful steps in alignment with our insights and understanding.

By fixing it you free yourself to be adaptable. You double down on agility. You pave the way for a future-ready business.

So the genre project was my "Gift for Tomorrow" project at Net-flix. What's the equivalent project in your environment? What's your "Gift for Tomorrow" project?

CHAPTER 6

Future-Ready Evolution

Digital transformation. It's a buzzword we often hear tossed around in boardrooms, conferences, and strategy sessions, usually associated with innovation, growth, and the future. But what does it truly mean to transform? And what if we have been getting it wrong?

One of the great misconceptions about digital transformation is that it starts with technology. This misguided approach may lead to the creation of technologies that, while advanced, may not align with human needs at all, and perhaps not even with business needs.

Imagine you are at a leadership summit, and a keynote speaker unveils the latest AI technology. It promises to revolutionize your industry, to leapfrog the competition, to woo untapped markets. The room buzzes with excitement; the impulse to invest is strong.

Reflect for a moment: Are you tempted? Or do you pause to ask: "Does this technology align with actions we should be prioritizing next that will have the greatest positive impact on our future?"

For many of us, technology has a magnetic pull. Shiny gadgets and groundbreaking software tantalize us with promises of instant *everything*. The allure of digital innovation hype cycles and splashy headlines can tempt us to believe tech can solve all our problems. But that belief can lead us astray, luring leaders to pour resources into the latest tech trend, only to realize it does not align with the needs of their team or customers. I've seen this firsthand. In their rush to keep up or get ahead, organizations can lose sight of their core purpose and values.

Technology, powerful though it is, is neither a magic bullet nor an all-powerful god. The problem is in how to embrace tech's potential without investing too much belief in it; how not to imbue it with supernatural powers.

I propose that we update the discussion of digital transformation—and its more proactive counterpart, innovation—to a holistic and adaptive approach of *future-ready evolution*. This blended approach to transformation and innovation requires us to continuously learn and adapt, while staying ahead of the curve by remaining true to our own sense of what matters. Think of it as *purpose at scale*. It's about understanding what it is we are trying to do as an organization, and extending the capacity of our organization beyond whatever limitations we may have.

Imagine with me: a world where every business, large and small, can leverage the technology needed to create more streamlined and robust future-ready operations, better poised to compete, and better able to evolve to offer increasingly meaningful human experiences. This is the Tech Humanist leader's advantage: business objectives, technological capabilities, and human outcomes all in future-ready alignment.

Jeans 2.0

If you mention the name Levi's, the image of rugged, hard-wearing denim jeans instantly pops into most people's minds. It's a 170-year-old brand that's woven into the fabric of American culture, as enduring as the riveted denim work pants it patented during the Gold Rush era.

But in the early 2000s, Levi-Strauss was struggling: sales were at an all-time low and the brand's golden glow was fading (Bergh 2018).

Enter Chip Bergh, the new CEO appointed by the board to breathe life back into the Levi-Strauss brand. Bergh, with his wealth of brand management experience at Procter & Gamble, was not afraid to roll up his sleeves and get to work. He wasn't a quick-fix kind of guy. Instead, he took the time to interview employees from across the company's hierarchy, revealing some key culprits: "a lack of urgency, of financial discipline, and of data discipline."

Armed with these insights, Bergh made difficult but necessary decisions. He replaced most of his direct reports early on. He also implemented slower, intentional changes, like setting up in-home visits to interview customers. This practice, picked up from his time at P&G, provided key insights that shaped the company's new brand strategy and internal culture. The result? The "Live in Levi's" messaging that endures today.

Bergh also saw the need for innovation. He relocated the company's innovation factory from Turkey to a few blocks from its headquarters in San Francisco. This decision not only reduced costs but also allowed for an iterative innovation experience, bringing designers and innovators together. With direct access to the tools they needed, Levi-Strauss Co. began to design denim that could compete with athleisure, the then-leader in women's apparel. The new designs featuring technologies such as four-way stretch were a hit, taking the company's annual sales from under $800 million to over $1 billion.

But Bergh did not stop there. He also embraced the digital transformation the company needed, investing in AI and predictive analytics. When the COVID-19 pandemic hit, and customers flocked to online ordering, Levi's was prepared. Thanks to prior investments in AI and predictive analytics, it optimized warehouse operations and launched curbside pickup at about 80% of its roughly 200 US-based stores (a choice that was only possible because of the company's reinvestment of revenue into brick-and-mortar in the years after Bergh's arrival, despite retail trending away from physical storefronts at the time).

The company's investment into digital had also paved the way for a new C-suite role in 2019: chief global strategy and AI officer, created for Katia Walsh, whose extensive background in data and analytics prepared her to integrate digital, data, and AI competencies into the company's global strategy and growth initiatives. That foresight helped the company offer targeted promotions, running a campaign throughout Europe in 2020 that achieved sales five times higher than the previous year.

As Chip Bergh retired in 2024, he left behind a legacy of transformation and innovation. He turned around a brand that was struggling and made it a leader once again. But more importantly, he did

it by focusing on people—employees, customers, and consumers—
and by using technologies in a supportive, future-ready approach.

Unpacking the Meaning of Transformation

To be honest, after working in this space for a few decades, I take
issue with the term "digital transformation." Well, *two* issues: the
word "digital" and the word "transformation."

The term "digital" suggests a mere shift from analog, reminiscent
of replacing old-fashioned alarm clocks with digital ones, like the
one Bill Murray endlessly smashed in *Groundhog Day*. At one point,
this shift was revolutionary, but now, it's old news.

When technologies such as AI, blockchain, or virtual reality
become increasingly prevalent in the experiences within your industry, that's an external force putting pressure on your priorities. When
COVID happened, and restaurants needed to be able to provide
more flexible online ordering capabilities, that was a major external force. That goes double what COVID meant for health care, of
course, or education.

So **digital transformation**, a buzzword we have been discussing for over 20 years, is what we say we are doing when we are
catching up to these externalities. In contrast, when we are striving
to *think ahead* of these externalities, we tend to call that process
innovation. Note that both processes are likely to be happening at
any given time in any given organization.

But all of that is still part of my problem with the term "digital
transformation." Because within the context of today's business environment what we mean is *data* transformation. We're talking about
collecting data from disparate parts of the organization and making
it usable so that we can make more informed decisions. This data
offers some of the partial answers that we are going to be using
to understand the insights required to form strategies, to develop
timely approaches, and to bank the foresights that will help us shape
the future.

But even that is misleading, because *data is fundamentally about
people*. It's about understanding what people want, their relationships with one another, how they interact with your website or move

through a store, what products they have purchased or will need to purchase again. Essentially, it's about identifying people's needs and what is meaningful to them.

As for "transformation," it's a word loaded with profound connotations, evoking images of sweeping changes, but its usage here feels too abstract, too clinical. Too trite. When I look at my own life, I appreciate that transformation has been a constant theme, shaping me and my journey in countless ways.

From changing careers to reinventing myself, from adapting to personal upheavals to navigating professional challenges, transformation has always been at the heart of my experiences. It's not just about the big, flashy changes but also about the subtle, often unnoticed shifts that guide us toward new paths and possibilities.

Personal Transformations: The Heart of Change

Consider the moments of personal change—the times when life throws us curveballs, and we are forced to rethink our direction. Tragedies, personal growth, and the unexpected twists of fate compel us to transform, to adjust our vision of what life looks like after such experiences. These transformations are deeply personal and often painful, but they are also the ones that lead to the most profound growth.

For instance, in my own life I have experienced significant personal losses—among them the deaths of my father and my first husband—and these losses shook my world. They brought on periods of intense grief and confusion, but they also became powerful catalysts for transformation. Through adapting after each loss, I started to see life a little differently, reevaluating my priorities and redefining my goals. This personal transformation wasn't easy, but it was necessary. It taught me resilience, empathy, and the importance of embracing change.

The skill we learn from transformation is how to figure out what life is going to look like afterward, and the willingness to make the necessary changes, no matter how grueling or initially unwanted. That's why many of my favorite people are those who have likewise been through many transformations of their own.

Professional Transformations: The Business of Change

Professionally, my focus has long been on the kind of transformation that happens in business. I've seen firsthand how companies must constantly evolve to stay relevant. Business transformation is not just about adopting new technologies or restructuring teams; it's about rethinking strategies, embracing innovation, and staying ahead of the curve.

Interestingly, the lessons from personal transformations often apply to professional ones. Both require openness to reality, the ability to assess the circumstances, and the willingness to think forward in ways that break from the past. The same principles of resilience, adaptability, and forward-thinking apply, whether you are navigating a personal loss or leading a business through a market shift.

Experience-Driven Transformation

Of course, technology goes through transformations, too. Think: What's the most mind-blowing thing you have seen technology do?

You may picture the Boston Dynamics robot demonstration videos. You might think of space shuttle launches. Some of you might recall something ChatGPT did just this week.

My whole tech career has been one long series of tingles-on-the-back-of-the-neck moments. Augmented reality. Artificial intelligence. Robots. Rocket launches. Carrying my entire music collection in my pocket. Carrying my entire book collection in my pocket. Carrying a supercomputer more powerful than the one we used for landing on the moon in my pocket.

But it's also mind-blowing the way the experiences have evolved, for example, the fact that I can now, as I walk the streets of Manhattan, preorder a Starbucks on my phone, customized to my whims, pay for the coffee and tip the barista with a button press, and then walk into the store and swoop it right off the counter with just a thank-you and a smile.

The most influential innovations stem from a deep understanding of human experience. Not business objectives, although these must align, because these are too abstracted from human thriving. Not tech capabilities, although these should also align, because they are too arbitrary to offer guidance. As humans, it only makes sense to start from a human orientation, grounded in what we can experience—in human nature, if you will. This grounding means alignment with the larger natural ecosystem, as well. It should not be our intention to have humanity flourish while the rest of Earth collapses. Other than abandoning the planet or living in artificially controlled climates, that is not even a possible outcome.

Truly transformational technology never *starts* with technology. It starts with purpose. It's not about prioritizing the latest digital fad. It's about asking the right questions, extracting insights, and using them to guide our decision-making through the process of influential innovation across all areas.

Beyond Digital Transformation

Digital transformation is just one piece of a much larger puzzle that includes adapting to various forms of change. For example, workplaces and jobs are evolving faster than ever. Remote work, hybrid models, and flexible schedules are now the norm, and in combination with a greater push toward automation, this leaves open many questions about the skills and talent needed for the future.

Culture, too, is transforming all around us. Organizations have been recognizing the need for greater diversity and inclusion. An understanding of self-care and mental health have become more normalized. Our work cultures also reflect societal changes at large, and we have to adapt to ensure we remain relevant and aligned.

But there are still more facets to transformation: shifts in business models and supply chains. The emotional response people within an organization feel to change and the behavior that accompanies it. Very often digital transformation projects overlook the fundamental needs of change management at the human level. For example, say we introduce a new state-of-the-art enterprise system. Say it means that Sally is no longer signing off on a workflow she used to be the gatekeeper for, and now Bob is involved somewhere earlier in the process than before, and so on. Sally and Bob often—justifiably or not—experience fear and anxiety about the change taking place around them. It does not help that managers do not always communicate well around transformation.

Why Might Transformation Projects Fail?

In boardrooms and executive keynotes, you will often encounter the oft-cited statistic that 70% of digital transformation projects fail.

The origins of that benchmark have been debated and disputed: maybe it was Michael Hammer and James Champy in *Reengineering the Corporation*; some say it originated with John Kotter. On some level the truth does not matter. Ask anyone who has been part of enough complex, large-scale transformation projects, and they'll tell you: the number *feels* right.

While pinpointing the exact percentage of successful versus failed projects may be challenging, there are undoubtedly common factors in those that work out versus those that do not. In my own work, I've observed patterns that suggest a risk of failure. When employees resist a project, it often indicates a lack of communication and support from management. Engaged and empowered employees are the greatest assets a transformation program can have.

When I encounter suspicion and anxiety among team members, it usually means the executive vision has not been effectively conveyed. Addressing questions about alignment can significantly facilitate coordination across units and teams. Think of it like trying to assemble a puzzle without seeing the picture on the box. Providing that vision helps everyone see where their piece fits.

When planned deadlines and budgets are significantly off, it points to a lack of cohesive strategy and inadequate resource allocation. These factors are identifiable and, more importantly, addressable.

Our efforts can also be derailed when we have not adequately addressed the ethical concerns that are too often waved away as unimportant. Particularly given the rise of AI and data-driven technologies, questions are bound to arise about privacy, bias, and the broader societal impact.

Digital Transformation Canvas 2.0

Years ago, while writing *Tech Humanist*, I introduced the Strategy Articulation Canvas for Human-Centric Digital Transformation (Figure 6.1). This model has since helped leaders worldwide navigate transformation and innovation projects in ways that align their focus, purpose, values, and resources.

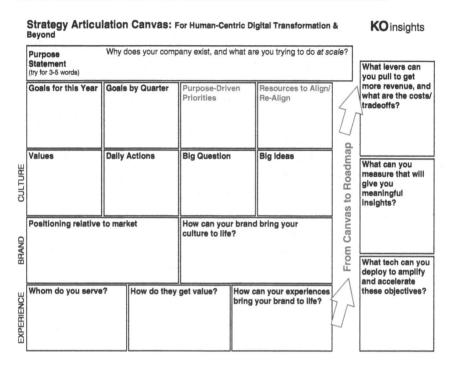

Figure 6.1 Strategy Articulation Canvas for Human-Centric Digital Transformation.

One technology organization in Hong Kong used the canvas to lead a massive organizational overhaul. The CEO wrote to me a few months after I'd presented it in a workshop there and told me that by focusing as a team on their purpose and values, they identified key areas where technology could genuinely enhance their mission. The result? A successful reinvention that resonated with both employees and customers.

The model in this canvas asks you to articulate your strategic purpose—as in, why does your company exist, and what are you trying to do *at scale?*—in just three to five words. The limit is important because it forces us to *choose only meaningful words.*

Once we have that articulation, we can work our way through the canvas, using this clarity to review our goals, values, culture, brand, and experience—all before we turn our attention to the data we collect and the technology we use to accelerate and amplify our objectives.

Aligning technology with our core values and purpose is essential for meaningful transformation and innovation.

Transformation at Scale

As big as transformation is, it is not the whole story. Broader shifts are driven by numerous external factors. The rise of AI has brought on new types of exposure and risk. We need to think strategically about cybersecurity and fraud. At the same time, evolving regulations around data and AI at state and national levels necessitate a strategic approach to protecting sensitive information.

But in the most significant projects, the ones that shape the next 20 years, we must look beyond mere change to meaningful *impact*. And many of the change factors extend beyond data and technology. For instance, climate change is increasingly shaping how businesses plan for disruption, innovation, and resilience.

Relatedly, geopolitical dynamics and economic instability are other critical factors that drive transformation. Our decisions may need to be informed by shifting world powers and economic uncertainties, which can significantly affect our strategies and decisions. Understanding these dynamics allows us to anticipate changes and adapt proactively.

Moving Past Reactivity toward Foresight

You want genuine alignment with your customers and impact on the market—not to mention the world. The goal is to create more seamless, personalized, and frictionless experiences that meet people where they are. This means rethinking every stage of how people interact with your brand. Technology is one part of the equation. But your goal is to spend as much effort on innovation as you do on transformation, if not considerably more.

Of course it is not just one magical digital transformation project, and suddenly you are done. As the years go by and technology evolves, businesses must constantly adapt, update, align, and seek efficiencies in new ways. After all, everywhere that you are currently facing transformation to catch up was a place where an answer used to be current and correct.

This balance between foresight and adapting to current realities is key to future-ready evolution. Since innovation is not just about reacting to current trends but having the foresight to anticipate future needs, when we anticipate and prepare for the future through this type of future-ready evolution, we position ourselves as first movers in the market. This not only grants us a wider lens and longer view with more insights and learnings to accrue, but it also allows us to shape the market and the practices around us.

Siemens Chengdu Factory's Foresight

In business, as in life, change is inevitable. It's not something to fear or avoid but rather something to harness strategically. The Siemens Chengdu factory stands as a lesson in technological innovation and societal transformation. Siemens understood and accepted that transformation cannot be driven by capabilities alone. Theirs is a story of foresight, nimble adaptation, and commitment to sustainability. But more than anything, it's a testament to the power of effective change management and the resilience of leadership that dares to render itself obsolete. So what did they do? They embraced change by establishing a Transformation Office (TO), a dedicated team to manage change effectively. The TO was designed not as a permanent fixture but as a catalyst, aimed at instilling new capabilities and digital ways of working into every part of the organization.

The changes they introduced improved production output but also forged deeper connections between complex manufacturing systems and data flows throughout the factory network. The goal wasn't just to enhance efficiency but also to weave future-readiness into the organizational fabric, making the TO redundant in the process.

From Reactive to Proactive

The idea of a transformation office rendering itself obsolete may seem counterintuitive. But is not that the goal of any transformation process? To bring about a future so bright that we no longer need to react to change, but instead, we become the change.

Siemens Chengdu's journey is still in its early stages, but it already serves as a powerful example of a manufacturer that's setting the right starting point for scaling impact. In the past three years, Siemens' Chengdu factory saw a 92% growth in production output. Yet, it did not lose sight of its commitment to sustainability. It deployed a holistic digital energy management system, introduced AI-based automation to manage production waste, and applied eco-design features to enhance circularity and dematerialization. The result? A 24% reduction in unit product energy consumption and a 48% decrease in production waste.

So what can we take away from Siemens' story? In its best form, transformation is a reactive process that leads to a more proactive innovative culture.

Crafting Future-Ready Strategy with Through-Line Thinking

People crave clarity, and our strategies should offer it. Consider Daniel Kahneman's book *Thinking, Fast and Slow*, which illuminates how we can integrate fast, intuitive thinking with slower, more deliberate decision-making. In a similar way, using through-line thinking allows us to anchor our strategies in sound, ethical considerations.

A future-ready strategy is not about discarding the lessons of the past. Reflecting on the past provides us valuable lessons. Instead, it's about using these insights as a launching pad while keeping our eyes firmly fixed on the horizon, pondering what we owe to stakeholders of the future.

And this forward-thinking need not imply a transhumanist perspective that neglects the needs of people living today. Decisions about policy and interventions must prioritize the living, the here and now, the local, the near-at-hand. It is simply not feasible to plan for the future in a way that dictates current policies without consideration for present realities. But it means we make decisions today that are informed by a clear understanding of their long-term implications.

Consider how IBM navigated a major shift in the 1990s from hardware to services. They leveraged their rich history and technological expertise to inform their transformation but did not let it confine their vision. The result? IBM has remained a relevant player in the tech industry, offering pioneering AI solutions even today, showing us that history and future-readiness are not mutually exclusive.

Yet, our decisions *must* integrate the needs of those beyond our immediate sphere, in terms of both time and space, including future generations, and including society as a whole and the world at large. Future-ready evolution should yield healthier long-term outcomes for everyone, from the present moment to generations yet unborn.

Pivoting Harmful Inaction into Harm-Reducing Action at Scale

Every company, even the most successful ones, will meet moments of crisis. Sometimes it is through mismanagement and hubris; at other times external forces conspire. But even when missteps have led to significant harm, the leaders face a choice. One path leads to harmful inaction, denial, and avoidance. The other way forward—admittedly more challenging—leads to meaningful innovation and sustainable progress. One story offers a useful example of all of the above.

A Costly Scandal

In 2015, Volkswagen—long celebrated as an icon of innovation— found itself at the heart of a controversy. An emissions scandal revealed the company had manipulated EPA emissions tests, resulting in nitrogen oxide emissions 40 times higher than reported. This wasn't a minor error; it was a significant transgression. The fallout was enormous, costing Volkswagen a staggering $34.8 billion in fines, refits, and legal costs by 2024 (Reuters 2024).

Beyond these financial implications, the scandal severed public trust in the Volkswagen brand, as well as the trust Volkswagen had directly built with its customers and stakeholders. The company had to face the fact that their decision-making process, which had prioritized quick scaling over ethical considerations, had failed them. Aside from the costly lesson in the importance of honest and responsible decision-making, the legal issues had drained the company of billions of dollars that it could have invested in developing its electric-car future.

In the aftermath, Volkswagen had a choice to make. They could deny the gravity of their mistake and continue business as usual, continuing down a path of harmful inaction, or they could learn and adapt, choosing the path of meaningful action. They opted for the latter.

The Road to Redemption

In 2016, Volkswagen formed a Sustainability Council with the mission of transforming the company into a global leader in sustainable mobility (Oge 2022). This council, composed of diverse voices from the United Nations, former politicians, academics, and the Red Cross, agreed on a set of strategic changes. These included prioritizing decarbonization as a corporate strategy, shifting to clean e-mobility technology, and focusing on ethical, collaborative, and purpose-driven practices. Volkswagen committed to the goals of the Paris Agreement, aiming for carbon neutrality by 2050 (King 2024).

Volkswagen's commitment to these strategic changes went measurably beyond public relations diversion: by 2023, the company had delivered 771 100 all-electric vehicles, a 34.7% year-on-year rise. This was a clear signal that Volkswagen was not just talking about change but was actively working toward it.

Beware of Creating an IT Dumping Ground

Their road to redemption was not without its bumps. In 2020, Volkswagen launched CARIAD, an ambitious project aimed at building a "unified software architecture" for all company brands, intended to lead to production efficiencies and new revenue streams from tech licensing fees and subscriptions (Barsky 2023). But since technology enhances the capacity and potential of efforts to scale, that means that missteps can escalate rapidly into major problems due to the scale of global businesses. CARIAD quickly became a dumping ground for adrift IT projects, failed to meet key timeline and performance goals despite employing 6000 engineers, and received a scathing audit report from McKinsey consultants. After significant cash drain and delayed EV releases, the company was forced to replace most of CARIAD's board and C-suite.

Driving Responsible Scaling and Meaningful Innovation

Despite these challenges, Volkswagen continued to innovate and adapt in its commitment to sustainable practices. The company initiated a partnership with Umicore, a circular-materials technology company, to strengthen the supply chain for battery recycling and reduce commercial risk. A McKinsey report hailed this move as a testament to Volkswagen's commitment to responsible scaling in the transition to net zero (Bland et al. 2023).

Lessons Learned for Future-Readiness

What can we learn from Volkswagen's journey? The emissions scandal was a stark reminder of the consequences of inaction as well as a costly lesson in the importance of honesty and responsibility in decision-making.

But their journey also highlights the power of bold, progressive leadership in the face of adversity—even when that adversity is self-inflicted. Their pivot shows a moment of self-reflection, and the potential for meaningful transformation and innovation when companies commit to sustainable practices.

It's never easy to learn these lessons in the harsh glare of public scrutiny. Making choices that are more ethically aligned *is* making choices that are more future-ready. Compromising on integrity will get you caught, slow you down, and cost you money and goodwill.

Transformation and Ethical Considerations

Transformation, therefore, becomes a complex calculus. It's not just about the needs of the many outweighing the needs of the few. It's about making decisions that drive growth and innovation while upholding the best of the principles that make us human—decency, justice, and opportunity.

When policies lack these values, extending them, codifying them into supporting algorithms, or embedding them into technology becomes difficult. Policies must be multifaceted, addressing a range of effects. For instance, while single-use plastics contribute significantly to waste, large-scale energy use has a more direct impact on greenhouse effects. Efforts must be comprehensive, covering various aspects of environmental sustainability.

Designing for Billions, Thinking for One

Designing experiences at scale seems like a daunting task. How do we cater to the needs of millions, even billions of potential users, while still keeping the service personal and human-friendly?

Our future-ready strategy requires both transformation to catch up with changes and innovation as our proactive stance, leading the charge and being the change. Both are likely to be happening in our organizations at any given time.

But how do we strike a balance? How do we lean into meaningful, human-impact innovation without losing our footing?

You start with the strategic articulation of your own purpose: what the company exists to do, what it is trying to do at scale. This is an essential orientation for everything that follows.

Then use technology to amplify the best of human experiences, making them more engaging, more personal, more human—with technology that is more human-informed, human-aware, and human-friendly.

The Power of Active Empathy

Innovation cannot wait for reactive data. We cannot just ask customers what they want. They might not know until they see it. So how do we innovate?

Understanding the people we serve is the cornerstone of designing human-friendly tech solutions. This involves more than just recognizing their needs and wants. It's about feeling their frustrations, identifying their pain points, and imagining how we can make their lives better. This is a strategic use of *active empathy*.

And this means humans doing *heart* work.

This is not something we can delegate to machines because it's not about AI pretending to understand through statistically probable outputs; it's about humans understanding each other as only humans can. It's about opening our hearts and minds, stepping into our customers' shoes, and moving from vague ideas to concrete opportunities to solve problems.

Casting the Right Net

The digital landscape is vast, but our aim is not to cast a wide net. It's about casting the right net. Who are the people whose lives we can improve? Can they access our service? We might aim to create network benefits that people can share within their circles. This strategic outreach is about using technology wisely to serve those we can truly help. We want to reach the right people, not just the most people.

Structured Solutions for Specific Problems

Our opportunities for transformation and innovation often come from specific use cases—highly specialized scenarios where technology solves intricate workflow issues. Addressing these opportunities requires a deep understanding of customer problems and their context. With this understanding in hand, we can build and offer structured, scalable solutions.

Balancing Specialization and Generalization

The future of AI is not a one-size-fits-all solution but a balance of specialization and generalization. AI transformation can provide both unstructured and structured solutions, catering to general and specific applications.

Many of the most transformative solutions in workplaces are going to be domain-specific and highly structured. They may use natural language prompting and conversational AI, but their training data and corpora will focus on corporate solutions. This allows AI to serve as a virtual assistant, managing scheduling and workflow for everyone in the organization.

By keeping these considerations at the forefront, we can create experiences at scale that have both meaning and impact. This is the way we build a future that's not just tech-ready, but human-ready.

Work Transformation

Work, too, has evolved. And management. Managers can monitor the app usage and keystrokes that employees generate at home. It's kind of creepy, but we can do it. On the other hand, we can streamline so many of our tasks that there are people working multiple jobs from home simultaneously. That's not the case for most people, of course—most people are working hard at one job and worried that intelligent automation is going to make their positions unnecessary. However, I do not think we know yet how true this is or is not and over what kind of time horizon. Are most of today's jobs likely to be replaced or changed by technology in 50 years? Heck yes. There are not many jobs from 50 years ago that look the same today, and things are changing faster now. But in five years? That's harder to say.

There's churn, though, and you can see examples of it everywhere: Klarna, the "buy now, pay later" financial services firm, announced in Feb 2024 that an AI-powered assistant was effectively doing the work of around 700 full-time customer service agents. The outplacement firm Challenger, Gray & Christmas reported in early 2024 that companies have directly attributed more than 4600 layoffs to AI in just the preceding six months or so and estimates that the full count of AI-related job cuts is likely higher.

So we have seen displacement happening in some fields and throughout the business landscape broadly, but we have also seen new jobs created by new technology.

The question will be whether one keeps up with the other and whether we have the necessary upskilling and reskilling programs to help people transform out of old jobs and into newly created ones.

Cycle of Inquiry

How do we know we are capable of being the first to do something no one else has done? And how do we ensure we are not bringing about bad outcomes?

Consider Amazon Go, the "just walk out" grocery model, where because of sensors that automatically charge customers for what they take off the shelves, people are discouraged from getting items off the shelf for others. A seemingly benign rule, but one that asks people to abstain from helping one another. Moreover, because this is a common act, this is asking people to behave unnaturally. Plenty of humans were involved in the development of that platform who might have said that's asking people to behave unnaturally, or to change behavior in a way that, at scale, does not necessarily lead to a better future.

How do we balance the scales between the promise of innovation and the potential for harm? A big part of the answer is in practicing active empathy, understanding and validating the feelings and perspectives of team members, customers, and other stakeholders. Cultivating that kind of diversity and inclusion in the process, recognizing the value of different viewpoints, adds value. After all, a wealth of perspectives can only enrich the innovative process.

The journey to meaningful innovation is spurred by a cycle of inquiry. By asking the right questions, we can extract insights that guide our decision-making processes. The answers we seek are often already embedded within these questions.

Our mission, then, is to ensure that our questions lead to thoughtful partial answers that can inform insights, and—more importantly—to better questions.

The first question to ask is, **Why do we want to innovate?**

Is it because we see an opportunity in being ready with novel approaches? This may be so, but it's important to remember that educating the market about our innovation can be costly.

Or is it because we fear being left behind? It's a valid concern, but only if we are following where the rest of the market is going—which is more like transformation.

Perhaps then, we want to innovate because we believe there's a better way, and we are determined to find it. Or maybe, just maybe, it's because innovation brings us hope for the future. In a world full of uncertainties, every new idea feels like a beacon of possibility (Figure 6.2).

In our pursuit of truly powerful innovation, we must confront our assumptions. We need to ask: Is this technology ethical? Is it just? Is it aligned with our values?

Innovation is about more than just technology or novel business models—at least the best examples of it always have been. Those have always been about leading with integrity, making decisions that are ethical and principled, bold yet thoughtful, progressive yet grounded.

The best models of innovation are transparent and accountable: clear about their data practices, and responsible for the consequences of their technological decisions. Remember, innovation is not just about "what's next." It's about what *matters* next. Innovation in a too-fast world demands courage, compassion, and conviction. It requires us to be adaptable, ready to pivot strategies as necessary, and promote a culture of continuous learning.

Optimization and Integration

A few years into my consulting career, I found myself sitting at a mahogany conference table, surrounded by a group of high-ranking executives, each more serious than the last. We were there to discuss strategies for enhancing their company's operations, and two words kept being thrown around the room: *optimization* and *integration*.

These both have their place, depending on the specific situation and objectives. Sometimes, it's more effective to focus on refining and improving what's already in place—in other words, to optimize. Maybe you want to refine what's already in place to enhance

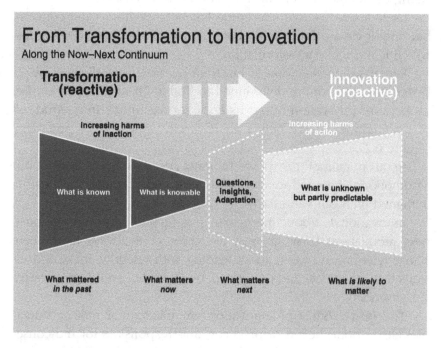

Figure 6.2 From transformation to innovation along the now-next continuum.

performance, reduce waste, or improve outcomes. In your organization this might mean streamlining operations, enhancing efficiency, or improving the quality of output. For example, a business might optimize its manufacturing process to reduce production time or materials waste. Or a software engineer might optimize a piece of code to make it run faster or require less memory. Optimization aims to make the most of existing resources and capabilities. It's the quest for "better."

My friend Phil M. Jones is the author of a book called *Exactly What to Say* about the big difference a few little words can have on your influence and impact. He often poses this question to a crowd: Which is better, "better" or "best"? He argues that it's better to be "better" than "best," as in "I tried my best." The latter implies an excuse, a limitation, a finite end to our vision and potential; the former is an always-on opportunity. We can always do better, be better, come up with better ways to work. We can improve our communication, our teamwork, our processes, our documentation and leave our projects, our teams, our organizations a little better than we found them. We can iterate our way to better results, better campaigns, better budgets. We can optimize our data management, our systems, our websites, our tracking. We can improve, we can polish, we can refine, we can level up.

And when we adopt that approach in continually revisiting the decisions we make for the future, we open the door to constantly creating opportunities beyond the limits of uncertainty. Our vision gets clearer, and we give ourselves advantages we would have never imagined possible if we'd only been striving for what we previously thought was "best."

Yet it's not an agnostic process. It requires a clear metric—a definitive answer to the question, "What are we measurably improving?" (If you are optimizing and you do not know what your metric is, try articulating it. Ask the question: If we get this more right today than tomorrow, what are we measurably improving?) Having a clear metric is a key indicator of having a clear purpose. Without this to guide us, our efforts risk becoming chaotic and undirected, leaving us lost in constant refinement.

Integration: The Bigger Picture

While optimization focuses on enhancing individual components, it can often be more beneficial to integrate—to bring together separate components for a more holistic solution. Integration looks at the grand scheme of things, aligning them to work in harmony. In business, this might involve unifying different departments or functions to improve communication and coordination. In technology, it could mean merging separate software systems so they can share data and work together seamlessly. The goal is to create a unified whole that's more than the sum of its parts.

But as I listened to those executives around the mahogany table that day, debating these strategies as if only one could be correct, a far bigger insight dawned on me: these concepts were not just about the balance between optimization and integration; they were a reflection of our attitudes toward technology and business—and even more, toward technology and humanity.

The challenge that gave birth to Tech Humanism was now apparent to me: the perceived dichotomy between technology and humanity. The truth, however, is that technology and humanity can coexist harmoniously—each enhancing the other, rather than being at odds.

It's a shame people so rarely talk about these concepts— optimization and integration, technology and humanity—together. Many of the most successful strategies involve a combined approach. We know what we are optimizing for, but why aren't we talking about the integrated holistic system we are operating within? Or we know what we are blending together, but we cannot say when or how it will be an improvement over the existing state.

The path to future-ready strategic evolution—that is both tech-ready and human-friendly—is not something we traverse only once and are done with. It requires both optimization toward a metric and integration of disparate systems effectively. It should empower us to align business objectives and human outcomes, amplified through technology, to create durable, resilient value.

Practical Steps for Leaders

So, how do we move from reactive transformation to beginning to foster a more integrative and meaningful approach to innovation?

Here are a few lessons to take away from what transformation has taught us:

1. **Embrace openness:** Be open to new ideas and perspectives. Look at challenges from different angles.
2. **Leverage data:** Use data to understand your people better, their needs, and their behaviors.
3. **Think forward:** Anticipate future trends and prepare for them. Innovation is not just about reacting but about preparing for what's next.
4. **Human-centric approach:** Always keep a sense of humanity at the forefront. Foster meaningfulness and other attributes that are part of human thriving.

Navigating transformative times toward a future-ready approach to innovation requires a blend of foresight, adaptability, and a keen understanding of the broader impacts of our actions. By making progress through meaningful steps aligned with insights and understanding, we can avoid unintended consequences and drive lasting, positive change.

Let us ask the tough questions, confront our assumptions, and align our tech initiatives with our values and purpose. In our quest for what matters next, let us lead with purpose, insights, and a deep understanding of the human experience.

As you reflect on your own leadership journey, consider the broader context in which you operate. Engage with your teams, communicate your vision clearly, and remain adaptable to the ever-changing landscape. By doing so, you'll not only navigate the challenges ahead but also inspire those around you to strive for greatness.

What Matters: Climate Action

While this book primarily focuses on navigating the delicate balance between current realities and future visions in the realm of tech decisions and digital transformation, its approach creates space for a broader dialogue—one that involves the pressing issues of our times, none more so than climate change.

At its core, the primary focus of this book is on the transformation brought about by technology, as a guide for leaders to the rapid change sweeping across industries. As this discussion has progressed, we have incorporated examples from the fields of climate and energy. These aren't random tangents. They are a recognition of the interconnectedness of our world today, where decisions about technology cannot be isolated from their wider implications on our environment, climate, and energy consumption. They are about acknowledging that the harms of inaction aren't limited to the realm of technology. They extend to our collective inaction on pressing global issues such as climate change, where the consequences of such inaction could be far-reaching, affecting our very survival.

I've been dedicated to this intersection in my work for a long time. In 2019, I had the chance to lead a panel of tech experts at the United Nations COP25 Climate Change Summit, discussing how we can use AI to combat climate change.

Including climate and energy examples in this book does not change its focus. It enhances it, making it more relevant and influential. The approach acknowledges that our decisions have a through line of consequences that go beyond our immediate context. They have a ripple effect, affecting not just our organizations but our society, our environment, our future.

What Matters: Sustainable Development Goals (SDGs)

What Tech Humanist leaders most often tell me they want is a world where sustainability is not just an add-on to our business strategies, but the very bedrock on which we build our future. This is why I advocate for using the Sustainable Development Goals (SDGs) as a clear and tangible road map toward a more promising tomorrow.

These goals offer both integration—a holistic system to work within—and optimization—clear metrics to strive for. They invite us to align our actions with them, ensuring the most substantial progress possible.

Have you ever stopped to consider how your work aligns with these 17 goals? It's like discovering a secret melody in a song you have heard a thousand times. Suddenly, you find your company's mission striking a chord with goals such as reduced inequalities, sustainable cities and communities, or perhaps industry, innovation, and infrastructure.

Many leaders already recognize this. Based on publicly available information as of 2022, 304 of the companies in the Fortune 500 have presented content relevant to aligning with the SDGs on their websites (Song 2022).

The SDGs are not just a list of nice-to-haves, but a powerful theme that can resonate with the work we are already doing. It's a way to orchestrate the efforts of all of us into what will make the most impact for the world.

What's even more powerful is that when we think about how we can apply technology to each of those areas, we can accelerate the work that we are doing and solve those problems, not just one by one but at scale. It's like turning up the volume on our efforts, amplifying our impact to reach every corner of the globe.

Sustainability is not just about environmentalism; it's a framework for progress, inviting us to align our actions to them, much like a 100-year company that's designed for durability, adaptability, and resilience. In other words, future-ready strategy *is* sustainable strategy: it's about having the foresight to create value now and ensure that value stands the test of time.

Decision Tool: Reflective Checklist for Meaningful Innovation

1. **Review promises and delivery relative to purpose:** Are our services living up to our promises? Do they align with our purpose? Are we continuously improving and adjusting based on feedback and results?
2. **Audit ethical practices:** Are we being transparent and maintaining integrity, even when under pressure? Are we holding ourselves accountable for our actions and their impacts?
3. **Consider global impacts:** Are our actions contributing to global tensions, or are they helping alleviate them? Are we aware of the geopolitical implications of our services?

4. **Evaluate environmental impact:** Are our actions adding to global issues, or are they mindful of the environment? Are we taking steps to minimize our impact?

5. **Reflect on decision-making practices:** Are we making decisions in a hasty, top-down manner, or are we taking an iterative, reflective approach that involves all stakeholders?

Integrating these considerations into your decision-making process fosters a culture of empathy, integrity, and sustainable innovation.

PART III

A Leader's Guide to the Future

CHAPTER 7

The Leadership That Matters Next

In many ways, today's work is already starting to look very different. We are seeing the rise of hybrid work models, with more people working remotely and an increase in the use of surveillance technologies to monitor workers. There is a shift happening in the balance of power between workers and employers, with workers becoming more aware of their agency and demanding more control over their work lives. And we are seeing the emergence of new types of work, such as the gig economy and the rise of the independent contractor.

It has also created opportunities for companies to rethink the way they do business on even a three- to five-year horizon—and for workers to reconsider their priorities in parallel.

We're creating the future of work with every decision we make today. So today and every day we have the chance to calibrate those decisions around our values. As we step into this new era, let us carry with us the principles that have always mattered: trust, empathy, and respect for the human spirit. While technology can shape our work, it is our values, our ethics, and our humanity that should shape our technology.

Because what matters next is not just what we achieve, but how we achieve it. It's our choice to make: not just what *work itself* will look like in 2030, but who *we will be* as leaders, as teams, and as human beings in that future.

Leadership in the age of technology and AI requires a human-centric approach. Technology is a means to an end, not an end in itself. It's about combining technical capabilities with ethical considerations. We must ask ourselves: Are we using technology to enhance human well-being? Are we making decisions that align with our values and ethics?

I've found that the most influential leaders are those who combine professional expertise with trust-building, a deep sense of empathy, and ethical responsibility. Because whether we look 5 years out or 50, these qualities are likely to continue to shape the human dynamics of the workplace.

The Invisible Currency of Work

In my first-ever week as the first-ever content manager at Netflix, I stumbled on a peculiar pattern. On certain days, a handful of team members would call out sick: three content producers on the same day. The same three a few days later. And then again, a few days after that. I was puzzling over the mysterious ailment that seemed to afflict them simultaneously until a coworker in another department kindly tipped me off:

"Check the surf report."

I did, and sure enough, the conditions had been prime for surfing on those days. As it turned out, my team members were passionate surfers.

The next day I gathered my team together and I asked about surfing. They were initially hesitant to open up to their new manager, but eventually they began to explain when they go out, how long they stay out, when they get back home—and we all saw how it could coexist with their work schedules. The solution was simple: they would surf early in the morning and come to work afterward. The result was a win-win. They got to enjoy a hobby they loved, and our team's productivity improved as half the team wasn't "sick" anymore. Above all, we established a vital element in our team dynamics: trust.

What this experience taught me as a manager about trust and team building is even more relevant in the era of growing remote and hybrid work. In a literal sense, of course, this is not a story about working remotely, because I was, in fact, asking my team to come into the office. But it is a story about acknowledging the reality of what people want and need, the kind of adaptability that feeds performance, and finding ways to be effective as a team that work for everyone.

Our surfing episode was a small but powerful lesson in trust and team building, lessons that have become critically important in today's world of remote and hybrid work models.

We are living in an era of Zoom meetings and asynchronous work, where trust between employers and employees is being stretched in unprecedented ways. Trust, however, is not a one-way street. It is a multidimensional bond between individuals, the faith managers have in their teams, the confidence employees have in their leaders, and the belief that the organization is secure and stable.

Employees and employers are navigating this new landscape, sometimes resulting in greater unionization and other times in passive disengagement leading to media-named trends such as "quiet quitting." Trust, or the lack of it, is at the heart of these changes.

Trust in the Digitally Transformed Age

Many of today's leaders are more familiar with a traditional work setup where we could walk around, interact with our teams, and glean insights from those casual hallway conversations. In this setting, trust was built on a combination of personal interactions and visible productivity. But what happens when the workplace is virtual, and your team is dispersed across different time zones?

As we navigate the rapidly evolving landscape of work, leaders and teams alike must overcome their discomfort to arrive at the best-fitting solutions. How can we build trust when we are not all in the same physical space? How do we foster a culture of accountability without resorting to invasive surveillance? To be fair, not enough managers have sufficient training in how to elicit the best work product in these environments or with distributed teams. And we have not given most managers nearly enough guidance on how to manage a work environment that is fundamentally a combination of humans and machine: "machine teaming" with automation-based efficiencies and human-based nuances, context, and emotional intelligence.

How We Show Up for Each Other

But we cultivate trust remotely the same way we cultivate trust in general: it begins with ***trustworthiness***. Leaders need to, well, lead—they need to go first, and not only create a *sense* of trustworthiness but *demonstrate* their trustworthiness. And a big part of that is **clarity**: clear communication, establishing shared purpose, managing expectations, and managing direction. When team members understand their role within these parameters, they can commit their best, whole selves to the challenge.

Another key component of trust-building is **transparency**. This involves being open about the "what" and "how" of decisions as well as taking responsibility for their outcomes. In a remote or hybrid work environment, transparency is even more critical as it helps bridge the physical gap and keeps everyone on the same page.

Transparency is one of the ways to address the productivity measurement challenges that tend to lead to unnecessary surveillance, too. When we set clear expectations and are transparent in how we will measure productivity, as well as how we collect, use, and safeguard data, we can make the decisions that affect our teams with a greater ethical integrity and alignment.

Other components to the challenges of building trust lie primarily across three key areas: **meaningful measures of work**, **clear expectations**, and **empathy**. We'll explore each in more detail.

Engaging in open conversations about the use of surveillance technology, for example, can help foster mutual understanding and trust. Leaders should not shy away from these discussions but instead, welcome them as opportunities for learning and growth. We'll discuss surveillance shortly.

Trust is not just about physical presence in the workplace; it's about committing wholly to a shared purpose and work standards. It's about showing up for each other, even in virtual spaces. This whole-hearted team dynamic can happen anywhere, provided the context is built on clear expectations, communication, and mutual respect.

Meaningful Measures of Work and Clear Expectations

In the Netflix surfing story, I did not determine my team's performance by the number of hours they spent in the office, but by their productivity and contribution. This is the first step to building trust—we need **meaningful measures of work and progress**. In many cases, this means shifting our focus beyond solely quantifiable outputs, such as lines of code, words written, or hours in the office, to include qualitative outcomes.

Particularly with knowledge work, people need a certain amount of white space to work in. In my days as a technical writer, I used to have a sign above my desk that said, "A writer is writing even when staring into space." Creativity can be messy. That's how we get to the magic.

Changing the emphasis from "how much" to "how well" reflects that we value people, not just processes. These micro-measures are a way of managing people like machines. And this tendency may increase the more we get used to having machines and automation in work environments.

Although one thing that becomes clearer in the age of increased tech-augmented human work and human-augmented automation is that this duality makes assessment simpler. With machines and automation in general, we are measuring and optimizing. But human workers are not repeating processes to be optimized. Human workers add value, so our work should be *evaluated*—even that word itself gives us a robust clue. Increasingly, the work we do should be adding *value* over and above the mechanics of our contribution, in alignment with the *values* of the organization. And that means our work output can be *evaluated* for its quality and adherence to the standards we established.

Right now we are talking primarily about knowledge work, but if we look at people doing other types of labor that is more manual and repetitive, the insight still applies: we have to be sure we are managing to the right measures and optimizing for the right things.

In fact many manual and repetitive job roles, such as pickers and packers in Amazon warehouses, are increasingly driven—we can say "managed" if we include the quotes, at least for now—by algorithms. What that means is that if you are working in a warehouse and all the other people doing the same job type are averaging seven seconds to pick and pack, then you are expected to average seven seconds too. But if the other people start to go faster, and now the algorithm says you should do this in 6.42 seconds, you are going to have to pick up your pace to 6.42 seconds. Increasing your speed to this arbitrary new rate may mean skipping a step that ensures safety, thought, or quality.

Wherever we are managing work, we need to be sure we are optimizing for the right things. And in any case, we should be careful to articulate what is meaningful about what we are measuring. In general, efficiency is for processes. When it comes to people and productivity, efficiency should not be the leading measure.

People contribute to processes, but what they contribute to those processes is often of higher value than efficiency: it's good judgment, context, decision-making, knowing when something needs to be slowed down or stopped to prevent damage—which is not efficient in the short term, but far more effective in the long term.

Whatever humans are being measured for that only comes down to efficiency is almost guaranteed to be replaced by machines. And that's not such bad news. In most cases, we need to recognize and cultivate the higher value that humans bring to the work around those tasks and processes, though, which is where the new jobs of the future likely come in. And setting clear expectations around the work will help to make this entire process possible.

A Culture of Empathy

Finally, we need to cultivate a culture of empathy and understanding. Acknowledging and validating the feelings and perspectives of our team members is key to fostering trust. After all, our teams are not just cogs in a machine, but human beings with their own thoughts, emotions, and experiences. We need to acknowledge the reality of what people want and need to flourish and find ways to be effective as a team that work for everyone. Since empathy is such a critical component both of good leadership and of human-friendly tech decisions, we'll explore it more fully.

Leading with Perspective and Empathy

Much of the popular discourse would suggest that empathy, a cognitive tool often underestimated, plays a pivotal role in leading in a way that's human centered. But how does it enter into decision-making?

In an enlightening conversation with Dr. Kirstin Ferguson, a globally recognized leadership expert and author of *Head and Heart: The Art of Modern Leadership*, she proposed an answer: leading with both analytical intelligence (the head) and emotional intelligence (the heart). "Regardless of the situation, whether it's ethics and integrity issues or an employee issue or a budgeting issue, you have to bring balance," she says.

Empathy Coupled with Curiosity for Tech Humanist Leadership

Dr. Ferguson believes that leaders must be genuinely curious about the lives of people quite different from them to lead with empathy. This is especially important in a world where technology often amplifies differences.

She also suggested that while the technical side of leadership can be outsourced to AI and other technologies, the heart side cannot be replaced. The key here is empathy, a fundamental attribute in leading diverse teams and making inclusive decisions.

Empathy in Decision-Making

Unlike Dr. Ferguson's model, which is robust and nuanced, the popular discourse around empathy can often be one-dimensional. As you encounter headlines about empathy in leadership and decision-making, it may help to know a few key things. First, our cognitive biases can sometimes get in the way of good decision-making even in the soft and fuzzy world of empathy. There is a cognitive bias known as the "empathy gap," which can hinder future-ready and ethical decision-making. This gap is characterized by our tendency to underestimate the role that different mental states and emotions have in our thinking. Consequently, we make decisions based on short-term moods instead of considering how our future selves will feel.

Second, studies have found that it may also be easiest to conjure up empathy for people who look like us, who are attractive, and who are non-threatening and familiar—the sum of which can present a challenge to diversity (Bloom 2017). Given this, it's perhaps best to resist the urge to view empathy as a solo superpower. It would be more helpful to view empathy as a useful tool when intentionally decoupled from our unconscious biases and put into practice with a head-based attribute. Luckily, in Dr. Ferguson's research, she found this very correlation.

In studying leadership attributes, Dr. Ferguson found that *perspective*, a head-based attribute that's all about seeing a few steps ahead, correlates most highly with empathy, a heart-based attribute. This correlation is particularly relevant in our consideration of tech-scaled solutions and in business decision-making in general. As she said, "That's because if you are able to read a room, you can also see who's missing from the room and what is not being included or what diverse views aren't being heard." To create technologies that serve diverse user bases and make ethical decisions, we need to be mindful of whose voices are missing from the room. It is not enough for diverse views to be heard; in our efforts to make ethical decisions around human-centric and future-ready technologies, diverse views must be actively sought out and considered. After all, inclusion *is* a form of human-centricity; inclusion *is* a form of future-readiness.

The Role of Empathetic Leadership in a Tech-Heavy World

As Dr. Ferguson so eloquently put it, "The art of modern leadership" lies in knowing what is needed and when. As we navigate the balance between current realities and future visions, we must also strive to lead with both head and heart, making sure that our decisions are both analytically sound and emotionally intelligent.

What we tend to find, too, is that learning to integrate seemingly conflicting perspectives gives us the superpower of being able to do it again and again. And we do have more integration to do. We also need to guide our organizations toward a future that is not only technologically advanced but also socially equitable and environmentally conscious.

Because of the too-fast acceleration of unforeseen consequences, leading with empathy in a tech-driven age is not a nice-to-have but a necessity. With the right balance of head and heart, we can navigate our organizations toward a future that is not only technologically advanced, but also socially equitable and environmentally conscious.

Moreover, as Dr. Ferguson reminded us, while technology can guide us, it is our human qualities—our empathy, our curiosity, our capacity for understanding—that will ultimately determine our success.

Surveillance and the Paradox of Trust

While technology has enabled the shift to remote work, it has also brought new challenges. One of these is the rise of surveillance technology. While it can enhance productivity and security, it also raises ethical questions around privacy and autonomy.

In a conversation I had with Albert Fox Cahn, founder and executive director of the Surveillance Technology Oversight Project (S.T.O.P.) on *The Tech Humanist Show*, he spoke of workplace surveillance as "bad tech," endangering employees, giving employers undue power, and putting people at risk (O'Neill 2022).

The rise of surveillance technology in remote and hybrid work models presents a profound challenge for leaders: to strike the right balance between leveraging technology for business growth and preserving the trust and autonomy of their teams. This balance is not just about ensuring productivity or security; it's about honoring the very essence of what makes us human: our ability to think, create, and innovate in ways machines cannot.

Leading toward a Trustworthy Future

Technology must serve humanity's best interests. This means envisioning a future where AI not only enhances efficiency but also upholds ethical standards. But we cannot take for granted that the right outcomes will happen on their own. Trust in technology is not a given. We need to model and monitor what matters.

We do not examine enough the idea that in order to expect trust, your efforts must be *trustworthy*. What steps can we take today to build a trustworthy technological future?

Deepfakes, for example, which we discussed earlier, mimic reality so believably that they have the capacity to undermine trust in visual media, a cornerstone of modern communication.

How can we ensure that our AI systems are both advanced and ethical? Building trust in AI is about creating systems that are transparent, ethical, and reliable. That means taking meaningful steps in alignment with insights and understanding, right down to the level of data strategy. This requires transparency—being very open about how data is collected, used, and protected. Doing so will make biases and weighting clearer in ways that make technology more useful.

Take, for example, asking a friend for restaurant recommendations. Their suggestions will inevitably be shaped by their individual tastes and preferences. Just as you probably would not trust me, a longtime vegan, to recommend the best steakhouse in town, we need to understand that AI is prone to its own biases. It only "knows" what it has been trained to know. This leads us to a complex question: How can we trust AI's suggestions knowing they are shaped by its inherent biases?

The issue of bias is further complicated when we consider how the weightings and preferences in our decisions today may serve us tomorrow. Standards evolve with the times; for example, the gender norms that society followed even two to three decades ago do not have much relevance today. As we progress into the future, what used to seem like weighting may devolve into bias, leading to different societal outcomes.

Moving forward, there may be no way for you to know all of the ways your data collection strategies might be putting your business, employees, customers, and users at risk, so in some cases the best thing to do is to either collect less data, or find ways to mitigate your own access to it so that there is not a way for police agencies or local governments to force you to give it up.

Trustworthy data use is not just about compliance; it's about aligning with the values and expectations of those we serve.

Building Trust into Tech: Actionable Steps

Trust is not just a technical challenge; it's a fundamentally human one. So how do we build trust into our tech and processes? Here are a few actionable steps:

- ◆ **Data audits:** Regular data audits can help identify and rectify discrepancies, ensuring data integrity and showing our commitment to accuracy and reliability.

- ◆ **Verification programs:** Implementing robust verification programs can build a layer of trust by ensuring that the content we interact with is authentic, reducing the risk of deception.
- ◆ **Media literacy:** Educating the public about media literacy can equip them to discern truth from fiction, identify untrustworthy content, and feel more confident in navigating the digital landscape. Media literacy programs help foster a more trusting and informed community.
- ◆ **Digital citizenship:** Promoting responsible digital citizenship can encourage ethical behavior online, contributing to a more trustworthy digital environment.
- ◆ **Decision transparency:** Making AI decision-making processes transparent can demystify how decisions are made. Transparency is not just a technical feature; it's a bridge to trust.

How Much Management Should We Delegate to Algorithms?

Imagine you are in charge of hiring at a company as colossal as Amazon, with over half a million employees globally. You're faced with the mammoth task of sifting through an ocean of resumes to select the most promising candidates. It seems only logical to develop an AI tool to automate the process, right? This is precisely what Amazon set out to do in 2014, hoping to streamline the recruitment process and spot talent more effectively. But as we explore this case, we'll see how it uncovers some intriguing ethical considerations of data-driven, AI-optimized business environments.

But before the tool can help you spot talent, you have to train it with a starting database. You want it to pick rising stars. No problem: you have a huge cache of résumés that were submitted over the previous 10 years. *And* you know which of those résumés led to a hire. Heck, you even know which of those went on to become top performers, which means you can screen résumés for similarities to those winners. With hundreds of ranking factors, the tool can model the success of those hires to screen for tens of thousands of terms or traits.

You can set the tool to crawl the web, identify potential candidates, and rank them based on how well they match up to this database of résumés submitted over a decade. On paper, it sounds like a brilliant innovation, does not it?

Some problems creep up, though. You're in tech. Tech has long been a male-dominated field. That means that an awful lot of the résumés you have were bound to have been submitted by men. A disproportionate percentage of the people *hired* from that set of résumés were bound to be men. And in fact, upon closer inspection, it turns out your AI recruiting tool has refined itself to recognize résumés that belong to women because of, say, the presence of the word "women's" or the names of all-women colleges. And it's ranking those as less suitable.

You see the problem and step in—as Amazon did in 2015. You review the training data, editing the terms the tool can use to screen candidates, removing any obviously gendered language.

But now you have begun to worry. What if there are less obvious patterns that are leading to discrimination? What if the algorithms are biased against subtle cues of race or sexuality or religion? It seems very likely that you will not recognize every pattern that leads to biased results. Algorithmic pattern-finding can detect matches and anomalies that happen at such a subtle statistical level that the human eye just is not going to keep up with. How are you going to ensure that the hiring is bias-free?

You likely cannot.

By 2018, Amazon abandoned the project, using the tool only as a reference point in their recruitment process. Nevertheless, it still serves as an important case study for businesses worldwide. And it mirrors other instances where delegating decisions to machine learning comes back with potentially problematic results. For instance, IBM's Watson, which helps in diagnosing cancer, may inadvertently develop biases based on the data it's trained on, potentially leading to unequal health care outcomes. Tesla's self-driving cars are another example, where decisions on prioritizing passenger versus pedestrian safety in unavoidable accidents pose ethical dilemmas.

The Amazon case illustrates the argument in favor of maintaining a "human in the loop" in decision-making processes. Relying solely on AI models for critical decisions is risky due to the potential for bias and discrimination. Auditing inputs, algorithmic processes, outputs, and the resulting decisions help to ensure the technology aligns with human-centric values.

In one of the more infamous stories in the machine learning space, Microsoft's chatbot Tay, designed to learn from Twitter interactions, ended up tweeting racist and offensive content—within days of its launch. This led to significant public backlash, as well as a healthy amount of ongoing ridicule.

The ethical responsibility of using AI systems in business is not just a theoretical concern. It has tangible, real-world implications on companies' reputations and bottom lines.

Future of Work Considerations

Consider upskilling. It's a little like updating your old smartphone. Sure, it works fine for calls and messages, but would not it be great if it could perform those advanced functions like the new models? As our workplaces transform, we all—from the intern to the CEO—need to polish our skills. This view of upskilling is about adaptability, about embracing changes in technology, culture, and more.

But let us not lose sight of what's at the heart of upskilling: the humans behind the tech skills. It's not just about learning to code or deciphering data. It's about fostering a culture of curiosity, resilience, and, dare I say, fun in facing new challenges. AI is both a driver of and a potential solution to the need for this upskilling, but our focus needs to be on the people first and foremost. After all, in the best work cultures, it's humans who drive technology to truly revolutionary results.

Because I often speak about the themes of the future of work, jobs, and the workplace, I also can field questions from a broad array of audiences, reflecting a wide range of concerns. Let us explore the themes of some of the most common questions that arise as we consider a future-ready approach so that our organizations and the people in them can thrive.

Humans and Machines in Harmony

Picture our future workplace. How will we manage teams of humans and machines in an environment where much is uncertain? The truth is, most managers have had little training on managing people, let alone teams of humans and machines. So how do we adapt to these demands?

One way we can begin to develop future-ready work processes that integrate humans with technology is by asking what helps each thrive. We know from multiple studies over many years that humans thrive on a clear sense of meaning, contributing to something bigger than themselves (Abid 2016). Machines, however, "thrive" by receiving clear and succinct instructions. Coincidentally, what leads to both is purpose.

By better articulating what it is we aim to do, what our values are, how we hope to matter, we can help both our human contributors and our technological augmenters do their best work. Leading the Tech Humanist workplace is going to require inspiring humans and aligning machines.

What's often missed in the conversations about the future of work and the future of jobs is that there is no singular future. There are *futures*, multiple and sometimes contradictory.

This is both because it is less useful to think of time and consequences as a series of deterministic inputs and outputs that trace from a moment in the past to a moment in the future, and because multiple contradictory things can be true at once.

So will there be job losses due to automation? Yes, it's happening, and it has happened in the past. But across every sector and job type? Not necessarily. Automation can also create jobs and enhance human performance.

It is also a truism often repeated that it is not always about AI replacing humans, per se; in many instances, humans using AI will displace those not using AI. This thought offers incentive for us all to learn relevant AI tools.

Purpose-Driven Workforces

As we have discussed with digital transformation in other contexts, the most egregious mistake we can make in transforming our internal workforce is to start with technology—to place tech at the forefront of the changes. In other words, for example, when we have a new AI procurement tool, it's tempting and understandable to focus our thinking on the tech: what jobs can be "outsourced," as it were, to AI. And then by figuring out where humans fit around it.

But we need to take a step back, or we may miss critical components of how we deliver value and how we can continue to do so in the future.

Whatever it is that AI can now do of what human workers used to do, there is process and impact from having that step automated. Do all the people upstream and downstream from that process understand the inputs and outputs of that process?

Here's where purpose serves as a central organizing idea because it is inherently a meaning-based—and therefore human-oriented—perspective. The gold-star question is: **What does your company *exist* to do, and what is it trying to do *at scale*?**

Zoom out to the strategic view of the organization: What does your organization do? What do your customers want from it? Where is the ***alignment*** between what success looks like in these objectives? How do experiences, brand, and culture serve to deliver on this purpose and alignment? The answers to these questions often highlight human values, as well as the value of human contribution. Once we have answered these questions we can identify the supporting resources, including technology, that can help amplify and accelerate this alignment.

As we step into an era where remote work blurs the lines between personal and professional lives, it's time to redefine our understanding of work. The essence of this shift is not just about being authentic at work but embracing an expanded concept of our "whole selves" at work. It's about recognizing that our productive selves are intertwined with our personal interests, our families, and our passions. Our "whole self" is woven from threads of all the aspects that define us beyond our professional roles.

As we adapt to this new understanding, we also witness a transition in workplace expectations. The regimented, process-driven approach of the Industrial Age is being replaced by a more compassionate, human-centric work environment. The focus is shifting from fitting into a predefined mold toward providing context, meaning, and emotional intelligence.

This shift is not just about improving employee well-being—it's also a smart business move. The closer a business aligns with human interests, the more potential it has to uplift humanity and contribute positively to the planet.

The Future Workplace

The integration of various concepts of place—such as the metaverse, remote work, and distributed teams—is an intrinsic part of this evolution. Virtual offices are becoming more prevalent, blurring the lines between physical and digital spaces in innovative ways. The convergence I wrote about in my 2016 book *Pixels and Place* is not just a distant concept but a reality that's taking shape as we race forward.

Adapting to these shifts demands a rethinking of traditional practices just as much as a willingness to explore new paradigms. The future workplace will require technological proficiency hand in hand with emotional intelligence. Decisions that shape culture and work need to be deeply informed by an understanding of human needs and desires.

Take, for example, a conversation I had with a CEO before a keynote. When asked about their remote work practices and return to office policies, the CEO's response was—shall we say—less than empathetic. His characterization made the employees sound like petulant toddlers rather than people who have a lot of logistical challenges to juggle in adapting to evolving work needs. In contrast, I hope your approach is compassionate and more attuned to the various needs of your people.

How we navigate cultural decisions like workplace policies hints at the approach we are taking with our overall decision-making and leadership.

The Human Experience in Virtual Workplaces

Like many technologies, the category of tools that fall under the banner of the metaverse have "varied practicality and appeal." But there is little doubt that much of our work world has migrated to virtual worlds and meeting spaces, even if we only mean Slack and Zoom.

These virtual environments demand that we pay even more attention to the human experience because we bring our full complement of emotions, needs, strengths, and flaws. Even when we use avatars to represent ourselves, we remain human.

And so does everyone else, for better or worse. This continuity of the human experience extends to both positive and negative interactions, as evidenced by instances of misconduct even in virtual settings.

In this evolving era, the challenge becomes creating spaces that not only meet the technical and spatial needs of tomorrow's workforce but also support and enhance the human experience today.

Preparing for the Near-Future Workplace

The landscape of the near-future workplace is poised for truly transformative changes, driven by post-pandemic realities, changing attitudes toward work, labor relations, and of course technology: from the threat as well as whatever the realities are of displacement by automation to the infrastructure that supports remote and hybrid work.

Understanding and adapting to these trends require a mindset that values flexibility, empathy, and resilience. By fostering a culture that prioritizes human-centric thinking, organizations can ensure that they are not just prepared for the future but are actively shaping it.

Integrating AI Meaningfully into Future-Ready Human Work

How can companies take advantage of the efficiencies of AI while respecting human values? Questions like this demand careful consideration, especially as AI and intelligent automation have altered the dynamic for numerous organizations.

The intersection of human and tech-related decisions can be complex. For instance, implementing a new HR policy such as remote work or compressed schedules requires considering technology needs such as videoconferencing, cloud storage, and cybersecurity.

Or consider an email campaign. It's easy to use AI to generate graphics and text, but does it further the campaign strategy? Does it align with what your customers expect from their experience?

Some organizations are doing a stellar job of restructuring work processes to capture this kind of emerging and evolving work product and the insights that come from doing it. Others, clearly, are struggling.

Of course, the opposite argument could be made! Plenty of smaller companies that could not afford—or did not have the skill—to put much strategic thought into the execution of their marketing and experience design will suddenly be leveling up.

But the most crucial aspect is that we identify what is meaningful about the experience. What *matters*? How do we amplify the most meaningful parts of the process? We must consider human fundamentals: time, place, meaning/purpose, connection. How will time change the message you are putting out? How will location alter the context in which someone receives it?

For example, I recall with perfect clarity waking up in a hotel room in Florida in 2011 to the news that an 8.9-magnitude earthquake (it was later revised to 9.0) had occurred outside Japan and that a tsunami was about to hit. As I watched the news in dread, I also watched social media and my email inbox, and cringed to see a series of marketing campaigns arrive, presumably prescheduled, with metaphors in their copy that were now unintentionally tasteless, like a "tidal wave of savings" and even a "tsunami of deals." The context of these marketing campaigns had dramatically altered overnight, yet no one had managed to pause them, or perhaps no one thought to.

As bad of a misstep as that was, it is still more likely that human editors and managers *will* catch that sort of error before it goes out than will AI. Because what that requires is a humanlike (or perhaps preferably: a human) understanding of the nuanced facets of human life, of society, of the tumult of human experience, and of how not to do or say the wrong thing at the wrong time. It is unlikely that AI tools will be good at this anytime soon. At some level, humanlike empathy is going to have to come from humans.

To navigate this landscape, we must rethink, reorganize, and consider: What are the ways by which people will continue to add value to the organization's mission?

Participative Leadership

As the pace of advancement in the world of technology and AI systems often seems to outrace our ability to fully grasp its implications, the question of ethical leadership becomes paramount. A key aspect of this leadership is the cultivation of a participative culture, one where every voice, from the intern to the C-suite, has a seat at the decision-making table.

Look at a company such as Spotify, for instance. They've disrupted the music industry by leveraging technology, while placing a strong emphasis on team collaboration in their decision-making processes. Their squads, tribes, chapters, and guilds model of organization ensures that everyone, from engineers to product owners, is involved in strategic decisions (Merryweather 2024). This approach fosters a sense of ownership and alignment with the company's core values, even when making complex decisions about AI and tech.

On the other hand, consider software company Basecamp. Known for its unconventional approach to work, Basecamp has often driven innovation by prioritizing team-wide discussions and collective decision-making. But when they made the move to ban political discussions at work, it was a decision made from top-down, and did not reflect what many of the team felt were core underlying issues that had less to do with partisan politics and more to do with the company itself (Newton 2021).

In the best examples, companies' strategic decisions are deeply woven with their core purpose and values. This is naturally going to be led at the top, but it is not solely a top-tier responsibility.

The key opportunity here is *participative leadership*—an approach that encourages employees to actively contribute to decision-making. This philosophy, rooted in social exchange theory and social cognitive theory, ensures that the unique knowledge and diverse perspectives of all team members are tapped into. Studies suggest that participative leadership will "dramatically improve the effectiveness of strategic decisions. By involving employees, leaders can leverage their knowledge and diverse perspectives to make more informed choices" (Wang, Hou, and Li 2022). Which means that larger teams *should* be part of future-ready technology planning anyway.

Teams develop their own sense of purpose. The most authentic articulation of why a company exists today and what they are striving to accomplish in the world can only be distilled from across the breadth of the effort. Input from all levels and all functions is essential. Also, when people across the company align their decisions with strategic purpose, they adopt transformations and innovations as their own. A collaborative process of articulation leads naturally to this sense of ownership and can account for nuances and details in executing against emerging ideas that management might otherwise miss.

When it comes to strategic decisions involving AI and other technologies, this approach becomes even more critical. For example, when IBM decided to focus on ethical AI, they did not just involve the top brass in the conversation. They proactively sought the expertise and perspectives of their entire team, thereby ensuring their AI ethics policy was both robust and inclusive.

Inclusivity and collaboration not only enhance the quality of decision-making but also foster a greater sense of ownership among team members. This, in turn, ensures that tech decisions are not just about chasing the next big thing but also about making choices that are human-friendly, ethical, and aligned with the company's core values.

So when we face the challenge of making tech decisions in a world moving too fast, let us remember to slow down, look around, and ensure all voices are heard. Because in the realm of AI and technology, the wisdom of many often outweighs the expertise of a few.

Influence without Authority

The reality of professional life is that title does not always match influence. So how can you lead change even when you are not the leader? This is a question many of us who are committed to change have faced; it takes strategy to exert a positive influence. What is your best approach if you are not the leader, but you want to make change?

The world has plenty of hills you can die on. The trick to winning some of the battles you choose, though, is to engage in only the most meaningful fights, and fewer of them. As the meme says, "Choose your battles. Choose fewer. That's still too many. Put one back."

In short, not to sound like a cynic, but for every battle you are inclined to pick, ask yourself: Is this going to be worth burning your political and social capital for? Far from being cynical, the question reflects two trade-offs: First, every stand you make costs personal energy, and you will want to preserve your energy for what's worth your investment. Second, it's a reality of work dynamics: if you want to be effective, you have to be flexible on most points, firm on just a few, and absolutely rigid only once in a while when it really counts.

Become known for what you care about. Are you most passionate about diversity? User experience? Including the voice of the customer in marketing? What do you care enough about to put your reputation at stake, and how can you demonstrate consistency in your commitment to become the reliable voice of this cause?

Throughout my career in contributor roles, I was the thorn in many a manager's side and a persistent voice among colleagues, tirelessly advocating for my chosen issues. I've also taken plenty of light-hearted ribbing about being a pain in the neck among my coworkers for not letting an issue die. But over time I learned to get more selective—and more effective.

My friend Liane Davey is author of *The Good Fight: Use Productive Conflict to Get Your Team and Organization Back on Track* and an expert in conflict at work. She points out that sometimes even when we appear to be backing down from an issue, we may still be holding a grudge. That will not be healthy for you, your team, *or* the outcome. As she says, "I see so many people claiming that they are 'picking their battles' when really they are just fighting an underground guerrilla war against the idea" (Davey 2024). If you cannot let your idea go, make sure you are doing your part to influence the decision in as many constructive ways as you can. One of the most important may be how you approach it.

When you are not the leader but want to effect change, it helps to master the art of relating. Try to frame your arguments from the perspective of the decision-makers, not merely your own. This approach requires you to deepen your understanding of the complexities not only of the issue, such as tech access or inclusion, but also of the arguments on the business side, and the ability to navigate between those perspectives smoothly.

Sometimes, despite your best efforts, progress may still elude you. If you still aren't having any influence and you believe the decision being made is wrong, it may be necessary to walk away. If you do, try not to see this outcome as a defeat, but rather as an informed choice made in the face of insurmountable obstacles. Your level-headed departure may end up being the loudest argument you could make for what you believe in—and it may even make enough of an impression to influence decisions that follow after you leave. After all, if our aim is to create a tech-ready and human-ready future, we are not trying to get mired in impossible battles, but we are trying to make progress using the best tools we can.

While leadership titles may vary, our capacity to influence change is not solely dictated by our roles. By carefully choosing your battles, understanding the art of relating, and recognizing when it's best to step away, we can all contribute to driving meaningful change.

Future-Ready Decision-Making for Leadership Legacy

Adding to the complex mental landscape for leaders is the notion of legacy. Your legacy reflects the decisions you make, the strategies you implement, and the change you foster.

In casual conversation about my work advising leaders about the human impacts of tech decisions for worse or for better, people sometimes ask me, "Do you honestly think leaders want to make a positive impact, though? Isn't it all about profit?" It's not an either-or, though. They are measured by profit margins and market shares—but they are driven by the desire to make a positive impact, to effect meaningful change. Out of the thousands of leaders I've met over the years of delivering keynote speeches at meetings and events, not one has impressed me as the kind of person who wants to leave a worse world behind them.

On the contrary, they often approach me to tell me how the ethical and responsible framework I'm presenting resonates with them and how they have been looking for just the right way to have this conversation with their board and C-suite. Every leader I've met, every conversation I've had, has reinforced my belief that most leaders, at their core, strive to leave a better world behind them. I'm glad that you are one of them, and that you have invested in reading this book to help you make the kind of decisions more likely to do just that.

Decision Tool: An Interactive Reflection on Purposeful Leadership

As we near the end of our journey together, I invite you to ponder some of the biggest questions:

Are we preparing our organizations for future challenges while addressing current inequalities? Are our innovations inclusive and equitable, or do they inadvertently widen the gap? In the pursuit of innovation, we must also ensure that we are not leaving anyone behind. We should strive to create solutions that cater to diverse needs and circumstances, from those living in underprivileged areas to those with disabilities. The spread of digital technology, for instance, should be matched with efforts to bridge the digital divide.

How can we balance ambition with accountability? In what ways can we ensure our technological advancements benefit all of humanity? As we innovate, we must also remain accountable for the consequences of our actions. This means considering the ethical implications of our technologies, assessing their potential impacts on society and the environment, and making necessary adjustments to mitigate harm. We must also be transparent in our processes and decisions, demonstrating to stakeholders that we are committed to acting responsibly.

This requires a holistic approach that considers all aspects of the innovation process, from the initial idea generation to the final implementation and beyond. It involves continuously learning, experimenting, iterating, and improving, always with an eye toward creating the most significant positive impact.

Here are some guidelines to consider on how to lead a culture of meaningful and integrative innovation:

1. **Establish a culture of trust:** Trust is the foundation of any successful organization. It empowers people to take risks, share ideas, and work collaboratively. Building trust requires transparency, consistency, and fairness. It involves keeping our promises, admitting our mistakes, and treating everyone with respect.

2. **Balance harms of action and harms of inaction to avoid unforeseen consequences:** Every action we take has potential consequences, both positive and negative. We need to carefully weigh these potential outcomes before making decisions, considering not only the immediate impact but also the long-term effects. This also means being prepared to adjust our course when unforeseen consequences arise.

3. **Foster the most meaningful human experiences:** Innovation is not just about creating new products or services. It's also about enhancing people's lives, making their experiences more enjoyable, fulfilling, and meaningful. This means designing solutions that resonate with people on a deep, emotional level, that meet their needs in intuitive and delightful ways and that contribute to their well-being and happiness.

Conclusion: Building a More Human-Friendly World

We have come so far, exploring how to address immediate realities and plan for future visions, weigh the harms of action and inaction, adopt an insights and foresights approach to decision-making, and move from backward-aligned transformation to forward-aligned innovation and future-readiness overall.

As we sticky-tape all of our maps into an atlas, standing on the precipice of a technological landscape we can now see and explore so much more clearly, our original question returns: Out of all of this, *what matters next?*

These last sections summarize the discussions into tools and models you can use with your teams.

Adopting Tech Humanist Principles to Lead the Way to What Matters Next

A brighter future that is not only tech-accelerated but also human-friendly begins with the Tech Humanist approach, where we align business objectives, human outcomes, and technological capabilities.

Key Tenets of Tech Humanist Leadership

1. **Purpose-driven:** Start with a clear strategic organizational purpose. Align it with the motivations of people both inside and outside the organization.
2. **Human-friendly scaling of technology:** Find the intersection between business objectives and human outcomes. This intersection is the opportunity space for ethical acceleration with technology.

3. **Human-centric future thinking:** When envisioning the future, begin with humans, not with technology. Align your focus, purpose, values, and resources within your organization and with the humans you serve as you undertake transformation and innovation initiatives.

4. **Consider human impacts:** In tech-infused business strategies, consider the impacts on humans. Technology should reflect and amplify human values, rather than undermining them. Remember the importance of scale and connectedness.

5. **Lead and decide:** Commit not just to a single decision or action, but to a journey of learning, adapting, and evolving for the sake of your purpose and your people.

These tenets guide individuals and organizations using technology toward making a positive impact on the world. After all, machines are what we encode of ourselves. For better *and* worse, AI models are our decisions writ large, including our values and biases, at scale.

Get clear on why you're doing what you're doing, what you're trying to do at scale. Be ready to deal with the consequences of scale by making better decisions, using AI and other tools well, and considering integrated, dimensional factors.

If we're going to be impatient, be impatient for *good*. Feel urgency around decisions that stand to create a more human future. A more sustainable future. A brighter future.

The Brighter Futures Challenge

After the publication of my previous book, *A Future So Bright*, I witnessed a shift in my clients' perspective. The challenge was straightforward but profound: How could they contribute to a brighter future in alignment with their business success, the success of their customers, and the United Nations Sustainable Development Goals (SDGs)? It was an invitation to step outside the confines of traditional business school strategy and venture into the realm of strategic optimism. This approach embraces the belief that business success and societal progress are not mutually exclusive but intertwined.

As I watched my clients embrace this challenge, I was amazed at the power of this shift in perspective. Companies that once solely focused on the bottom line began considering the wider societal implications of their actions. They publicly declared their chosen SDG in their social media bios. They started adopting more sustainable practices, examining their supply chains for ethical conflicts, and using technology to drive positive change rather than just profits. It was a powerful testament to the role businesses can play in shaping a better future, and it inspired me to explore this concept more deeply in *What Matters Next*.

However, as we've seen, this is not a one-time journey but a constantly shifting continuum where the decisions we make now have ripple effects that extend into the future. Technology plays a significant role, but it's not where we start. In our tech-driven world, it's all too easy to get caught up in the latest trends and advancements. But as I've learned through my years of consulting with companies such as Google and the United Nations, technology is not an end in itself. It's a tool, a means to an end. And that end, ultimately, is the fulfillment of purpose—whether at an organizational level, an individual level, or a societal level.

This realization becomes a game changer. I've watched it transform the way executives view technology. It has led numerous people to write to me to say they have adopted the view that technology can—and should—be used to improve human lives.

As we near the conclusion of *What Matters Next*, I invite you to continue your own journey by reflecting on your impact as a leader. How can you contribute to a brighter future? How can you leverage technology to drive not just business success, but societal progress as well? How can you become a leader who not only understands the concept of strategic optimism but embodies it? How can you shape your organization and the world for the leaders who will follow in your footsteps?

Aligning with History

In a too-fast world, it's more important than ever to make sure that, in as intentional a way as possible, your actions and choices are aligned with history. But aligning with history docs not mean being stuck in the past; it means seeing into the future. It means being the history we will wish to have been. It's a challenge to see beyond the immediate, to envision what's next, and to lead our organizations toward that future.

Let me share a story that encapsulates this idea. A few years ago, I was consulting with a utility platform that was rolling out a conversational AI platform. The company believed it would be more adaptable with more tech investment and fewer personnel. But rather than leaving their employees out in the cold, they trained those with particularly strong emotional intelligence to manage the AI responses, refining them and cultivating more of a sense of care and contextual awareness with each set of cases they handled.

On the surface, deploying a support platform that eliminated jobs seemed like a simple cost-cutting measure. And to be sure, it can be approached that way, but it's a missed opportunity. Because when we dug a little deeper, we found that it was an opportunity to reshape the company in a more human-centric manner. The leaders of this company understood that their decisions would shape the culture of their organization for years to come. They realized the importance of treating their employees with respect and dignity, even in the face of technological advancement. Together we surfaced the questions they needed to ask. What will the change mean in the long term? How will the company reshape without those jobs? What aspects of culture will that change? How will people remake themselves into the image of this new organization? Are there opportunities to reinvest some of the gains from that technology into training for some of the employees who were strong teammates, great assets to culture, or had leadership potential? Can they be part of adapting into new roles shaped by the platform?

This is the essence of aligning with history. It's about making decisions that not only serve our immediate needs but also set us up for future success. It's about weighing short-term gains against long-term implications. It's about understanding that every decision we make, no matter how small, is a step toward defining our legacy.

Consider the current discussions around climate change. There's almost no feasible legislation on the matter that will seem too aggressive in 10 years' time. More likely, anything we advocate for now will pale in comparison to the need we will recognize sooner rather than later.

Exponential technologies are similar. We are poorly equipped to visualize how rapidly these are changing the world around us. While comprehensive regulations and protections are evolving and are subjects for other discussions, the decisions leaders need to make are very much relevant to this one.

In every decision, there is an opportunity to align with history. There is an opportunity to shape the future in a way that reflects our values, our beliefs, and our vision for what's next.

In the grand scheme of things, some decisions matter more than others. But every decision, no matter how small, is a step toward defining our legacy. So, let's make them count. Let's make them matter. Because in the end, we have the opportunity not just to make history incidentally, but to align with it intentionally.

What we do today will echo through time, shaping the world we pass on to future generations. Our decisions have never mattered more.

A Tech Humanist's Guide to the Future

In some of my keynotes over the years as I have discussed meaning in the design and strategy of human experiences, I've alluded to a detail from the Douglas Adams classic, *The Hitchhiker's Guide to the Galaxy*, in which a supercomputer is built to determine the ultimate answer to life, the universe, and everything. After seven and a half million years of computing, it finally spits out an answer: 42.

A lot of people know that funny tidbit. The silly absurdity in the reductiveness of a numeral being all-meaningful is delightful—but that's not where this story ends. Over the decades since the book became a classic, many reader theories have emerged about why the number 42 just might have interesting connections to potentially meaningful interpretations. For example, if you add up the letters in "It's the answer to life, the universe, and everything" (not including spaces and punctuation), guess how many you'll count? That's right, 42.

That's not my favorite interpretation, though. By far my favorite meta-explanation is that in ASCII (American Standard Code for Information Interchange), which is the standard encoding for electronic communication, 42 happens to be the code for the *, or asterisk character. Perhaps you already know that in many programming contexts the asterisk is used as a wildcard character, which means it can mean *anything*.

That's not where this story ends, either.

On one occasion after a keynote in which I had recounted this story on stage, a woman who worked as an engineering lead in the organization I was hired to speak for approached me, holding an enamel pin shaped like a book on which was printed the title *The Hitchhiker's Guide to the Galaxy*. She said she had been in a bookstore the prior day and had seen this pin, and something about it had called out to her. So she bought it, not really knowing why, and had been carrying it around still in its cellophane packaging in her coat pocket. She handed it to me and said she was sure this was why she had been moved to buy it.

It was charming and moving and incredible. But even *that's* not where this story ends.

A good while later, this same woman sent me a note letting me know that soon after my talk she'd resigned from her job to go to work for an organization that uses data to solve world challenges. "I think and talk all the time about the example you shared. . . and the limitation it created to human interactions. . .. I wanted to make sure anything that I spend time working on would be the opposite of that example."

That's the story. It was her *what matters next* story. Perhaps now you have your own story.

Nothing has meaning that we don't put into it or take away from it. We each decide what has significance, what we decide to prioritize, what lessons we choose to take away.

Meaning is, always has been, and always will be what we make it.

The choices are—more now than ever—up to us. Perhaps we don't have all the knowledge we would like about why we're moved to make a choice we're making now, but since we must still act, we must make the best decisions we can, with both the present and future in mind. And with every choice we learn, we look for insights and wisdom, we collect foresights, and we try, always, to do better next time, and next time, and next time.

APPENDIX

Creating Your "What Matters Next" Action Plan

In alignment with the principles of Tech Humanist leadership and strategic optimism along with the many tools presented in *What Matters Next*, the following is a guide to creating your own action plan. You can also download a free printable template at whatmattersnextbook.com. This Action Plan draws from the principles of the now-next continuum and through-line thinking, providing a structured approach for decision-making in our too-fast world.

1. **Assess the known and the unknown:** Begin by identifying what you currently know and don't know. This includes existing knowledge about the current situation and any gaps in understanding that need to be filled.
2. **Identify learning opportunities:** From the unknowns, determine what could and should be learned. This might involve identifying key areas of uncertainty that could potentially be resolved through research or investigation.
3. **Create your now-next action plan:** Using the insights gained from the previous steps, devise an action plan that aims to minimize harm and fits within your timeline. This plan should include both immediate actions (the "now") and strategic steps for the future (the "next").

4. **Transition from transformation to innovation:** Start by addressing current needs and catching up where necessary (transformation). Then, move toward anticipating and preparing for future changes (innovation).

5. **Envision the future:** With the action plan in place, think more deeply about the future. Consider what foresights you already have. What changes do you anticipate? How can you prepare for them?

References

Abid, G. 2016. "How Does Thriving Matter at the Workplace." *International Journal of Economics, 4*(9), 521–527.

Ajder, H., G. Patrini, F. Vavalli, and L. Cullen. 2019. "The State of Deepfakes: Landscape, Threats, and Impact." Deeptrace. https://regmedia.co.uk/2019/10/08/deepfake_report.pdf.

Allsup, M., and L. Weinstein. 2023. "Seven Ways Utilities Are Exploring AI for the Grid." Latutude Media, October 14, 2023. https://www.latitudemedia.com/news/seven-ways-utilities-are-exploring-ai-for-the-grid.

Apple. 2022. "Empowering People to Live a Healthier Day: Innovation Using Apple Technology to Support Personal Health, Research, and Care." https://www.apple.com/newsroom/pdfs/Health-Report-October-2023.pdf.

Barsky, N. 2023. "Volkswagen Fires Tech C-Suite after 3 Avoidable Digital Strategy Errors." *Forbes*, June 2, 2023. https://www.forbes.com/sites/noahbarsky/2023/06/01/volkswagen-fires-tech-c-suite-after-3-avoidable-digital-strategy-errors/?sh=4f7fe075678e.

Bergh, C. 2018. "How Levi's Became Cool Again." *Harvard Business Review*, August 15, 2018. https://hbr.org/2018/07/the-ceo-of-levi-strauss-on-leading-an-iconic-brand-back-to-growth?registration=success.

Bland, R., L. Corb, A. Granskog, T. Nauclér, and G. Siccardo. 2023. "Scaling Green Businesses: Next Moves for Leaders." McKinsey & Company, March 10, 2023. https://www.mckinsey.com/capabilities/sustainability/our-insights/scaling-green-businesses-next-moves-for-leaders.

Bloom, P. 2017. "Empathy and Its Discontents." *Trends in Cognitive Sciences, 21*(1), 24–31. https://doi.org/10.1016/j.tics.2016.11.004.

"Code of Conduct – Alphabet Investor Relations" (2024, April 24). Alphabet Investor Relations. https://abc.xyz/investor/board-and-governance/code-of-conduct.

Alphabet. 2024. "Code of Conduct." Alphabet Investor Relations, April 24, 2024. https://abc.xyz/investor/board-and-governance/code-of-conduct.

Associated Press. 2019. "NY Regulator Investigating Apple Card for Possible Gender Bias." *NBC News*, November 10, 2019. https://www.nbcnews.com/tech/apple/ny-regulator-investigating-apple-card-possible-gender-bias-n1079581.

Baron, J., and G. P. Goodwin. 2020. "Consequences, Norms, and Inaction: A Critical Analysis." *Judgment and Decision Making, 15*(3), 421–442. https://doi.org/10.1017/S193029750000721X.

Bergen, B.K., 2012. *Louder Than Words: The New Science of How the Mind Makes Meaning*. Basic Books.

Botsman, R. 2022. "Tech Leaders Can Do More to Avoid Unintended Consequences." *Wired*, May 24, 2022. https://www.wired.com/story/technology-unintended-consequences/.

Brooks, A. W., and L. K. John. 2018. "The Surprising Power of Questions." *Harvard Business Review*, May-June 2018. https://hbr.org/2018/05/the-surprising-power-of-questions.

Burton, N. 2022. "Understanding the Causes of Our Sloth Can Help Us to Overcome It." *Psychology Today*. https://www.psychologytoday.com/intl/blog/hide-and-seek/201505/the-causes-of-laziness.

Carvalho, F. P. 2017. "Mining Industry and Sustainable Development: Time for Change." *Food and Energy Security, 6*(2), 61–77. https://doi.org/10.1002/fes3.109.

Chevallier, A., F. Dalsace, and J.-L. Barsoux. 2024. "The Art of Asking Questions." *Harvard Business Review*, May-June 2024. https://hbr.org/2024/05/the-art-of-asking-smarter-questions.

CMEPSP (Commission on the Measurement of Economic Performance and Social Progress). n.d. Home Page. https://web.archive.org/web/20150720212135/http://www.stiglitz-sen-fitoussi.fr/en/index.htm.

Davey, L. 2024. "Should You Pick Your Battles? – Part II." Liane Davey, April 7, 2024. https://lianedavey.com/should-you-pick-your-battles.

De Smet, A., G. Jost, and L. Weiss. 2019. "Three Keys to Faster, Better Decisions." *McKinsey Quarterly*, May 1, 2019. https://www.mckinsey.com/capabilities/people-and-organizational-performance/our-insights/three-keys-to-faster-better-decisions.

Desvousges, W. H., F. R. Johnson, R. W. Dunford, K. J. Boyle, S. P. Hudson, and K. N. Wilson. (2010). *Measuring Nonuse Damages Using Contingent Valuation: An Experimental Evaluation of Accuracy*, 2nd ed. RTI Press publication No. BK-0001-1009. Research Triangle Park, NC: RTI International. Retrieved September 6, 2024, from http://www.rti.org/rtipress. https://doi/org/10.3768/rtipress.2009.bk.0001.1009.

Eagleman, D. 2016. *The Brain*. Prestonpans, Scotland: Canongate Books.

EPA. 2021. "Helping Communities Manage Electronic Waste." US EPA, July 13, 2021. https://www.epa.gov/sciencematters/helping-communities-manage-electronic-waste.

Flanagan, M. n.d. *"AI and Environmental Challenges."* Environmental Innovations Initiative University of Pennsylvania. https://environment.upenn.edu/events-insights/news/ai-and-environmental-challenges.

Friedman, L. F. 2014. "IBM's Watson Supercomputer May Soon Be the Best Doctor in the World." Business Insider, April 22, 2014. https://www.businessinsider.com/ibms-watson-may-soon-be-the-best-doctor-in-the-world-2014-4.

Garfinkle, M. 2023. "'We Saw So Many Doctors': A Mother Says ChatGPT Accurately Diagnosed Her Son's Medical Condition After 17 Doctors Couldn't." *Entrepreneur*, September 12, 2023. https://www.entrepreneur.com/business-news/17-doctors-didnt-diagnose-her-sons-disorder-chatgpt-did/458927.

Gray, S. 2018. "Report: Google Employees Resigning over Controversial Pentagon Contract." *Fortune*, May 14, 2018. https://fortune.com/2018/05/14/report-google-employees-resign-pentagon-contract.

Hu, J. C. 2018. "Jeff Bezos Only Expects Himself to Make Three Good Decisions a Day." Quartz, September 14, 2018. https://qz.com/work/1390844/jeff-bezos-only-expects-himself-to-make-three-good-decisions-a-day.

Kanungo, A. 2023. "The Green Dilemma: Can AI Fulfil Its Potential without Harming the Environment?" Earth.org, July 18, 2023. https://earth.org/the-green-dilemma-can-ai-fulfil-its-potential-without-harming-the-environment.

Kavilanz, P. 2024. "Starbucks Sued for Alleged Deceptive Marketing of Its '100% Ethically' Sourced Coffee." CNN, January 10, 2024. https://www.cnn.com/2024/01/10/business/starbucks-lawsuit-deceptive-marketing/index.html.

King, C. 2024. "Mobility for Future Generations: VW's Sustainability Strategy." Sustainability Magazine, March 18, 2024. https://sustainabilitymag.com/articles/mobility-for-future-generations-vws-sustainability-strateg.

Kirkpatrick, D., 2010. *The Facebook Effect: The Inside Story of the Company That Is Connecting the World.* Simon and Schuster.

Knight, W. 2019. "The Apple Card Didn't 'See' Gender—and That's the Problem." *Wired,* November 19, 2019. https://www.wired.com/story/the-apple-card-didnt-see-genderand-thats-the-problem.

Kreutzer, V. n.d. "*Nikola Tesla.*" Institute for Consciousness Research. Edited by B. Viljakainen. https://www.icrcanada.org/research/literaryresearch/tesla.

Liu, Y., R. J. Dolan, Z. Kurth-Nelson, and T. E. Behrens. 2019. "Human Replay Spontaneously Reorganizes Experience." *Cell, 178*(3), 640–652.

Merone, L., K. Tsey, D. Russell, and C. Nagle. 2022. "Sex Inequalities in Medical Research: A Systematic Scoping Review of the literature." *Women's Health Reports, 3*(1), 49–59. https://doi.org/10.1089/whr.2021.0083.

Merryweather, E. 2024. "What Is the Spotify Model?" Product School. https://productschool.com/blog/product-fundamentals/spotify-model-scaling-agile.

Metcalfe, N. 2003. "Growth versus Lifespan: Perspectives from Evolutionary Ecology." *Experimental Gerontology, 38*(9), 935–940. https://doi.org/10.1016/s0531-5565(03)00159-1.

Milanesi, C. 2022. "In 2021, Women Filled 47% of U.S. Based Open Leadership Roles at Apple." *Forbes* March 23, 2022. https://www.forbes.com/sites/carolinamilanesi/2022/03/23/in-2021-women-filled-47-of-us-based-open-leadership-roles-at-apple/?sh = 3d0305ff2e45.

Mining.com. 2021. "A Breakdown of the Critical Metals in a Smartphone." https://www.mining.com/web/a-breakdown-of-the-critical-metals-in-a-smartphone.

Morris, R. 2018. "From Fossil Fuels to Green Energy: The Ørsted Story." London Business School, July 2, 2018. https://www.london.edu/think/iie-from-fossil-fuels-to-green-energy-the-orsted-story.

Mueller, J. S., S. Melwani, S., and J. A. Goncalo. 2011. "The Bias against Creativity." *Psychological Science, 23*(1), 13–17. https://doi.org/10.1177/0956797611421018.

Newton, C. 2021. "Behind the Controversy at Basecamp." The Verge, April 28, 2021. https://www.theverge.com/2021/4/27/22406673/basecamp-political-speech-policy-controversy.

Nordgren, A. 2022. "Artificial Intelligence and Climate Change: Ethical Issues." *Journal of Information, Communication and Ethics in Society, 21*(1), 1–15. https://doi.org/10.1108/jices-11-2021-0106.

NY DFS (New York Department of Financial Services). 2021. "Report on Apple Card Investigation." https://www.dfs.ny.gov/system/files/documents/2021/03/rpt_202103_apple_card_investigation.pdf.

Oge, M. T. 2022. "From Emissions Cheater to Climate Leader: VW's Journey from Dieselgate to Embracing E-Mobility." *Forbes*, December 6, 2022. https://www.forbes.com/sites/margooge/2022/12/05/from-emissions-cheater-to-climate-leader-vws-journey-from-dieselgate-to-embracing-e-mobility/?sh=2724489b2265.

O'Neill, K. 2022. "Interview with Albert Fox Cahn." *The Tech Humanist Show*, podcast audio, December 12, 2022. https://www.thetechhumanist.com/2022/12/12/what-does-spotify-unwrapped-have-to-do-with-surveillance.

O'Neill, K. 2024. "Technofeudalism: What Killed Capitalism with Yanis Varoufakis." *The Tech Humanist*, February 6, 2024. https://www.thetechhumanist.com/2024/02/06/technofeudalism-with-yanis-varoufakis.

Ørsted. 2022. "Danish Authorities Order Ørsted's Oil- and Coal-fired Power Stations Into Operation," October 20, 2022. https://orsted.com/en/media/news/2022/10/20221001568911.

Pilat, D., and S. Krastev. n.d. "*Why Do We Prefer Doing Something to Doing Nothing? The Action Bias, Explained.*" The Decision Lab. https://thedecisionlab.com/biases/action-bias.

Reuters. 2024. "Volkswagen Reaches $54 Million "Dieselgate" Settlement with Italian Owners." Reuters, May 15, 2024. https://www.reuters.com/business/autos-transportation/

volkswagen-reaches-54-million-dieselgate-settlement-with-italian-owners-2024-05-15.

Ross, J. 2009. "How to Ask Better Questions." *Harvard Business Review*, May 6, 2009. https://hbr.org/2009/05/real-leaders-ask.

Shearer, E., and K. E. Matsa. 2018. "News Use across Social Media Platforms 2018." Pew Research Center. https://www.pewresearch.org/journalism/2018/09/10/news-use-across-social-media-platforms-2018.

Song, L., X. Zhan, H. Zhang, M. Xu, J. Liu, and C. Zheng. "How Much Is Global Business Sectors Contributing to Sustainable Development Goals?" *Sustainable Horizons, 1* (2022): 100012. https://doi/org/10.1016/j.horiz.2022.100012.

Starbucks Corporation. 2021. "C.A.F.E. Practices: Starbucks Approach to Ethically Sourcing Coffee — Starbucks Stories." https://stories.starbucks.com/press/2020/cafe-practices-starbucks-approach-to-ethically-sourcing-coffee.

Steinbock, D. 2013. "Nokia's Failure: No Flexibility in US, Emerging Markets." CNBC, September 17, 2013. https://www.cnbc.com/2013/09/17/nokias-failure-no-flexibility-in-us-emerging-markets.html.

Telford, T. 2019. "Apple Card Algorithm Sparks Gender Bias Allegations against Goldman Sachs." *The Washington Post*, November 11, 2019. https://www.washingtonpost.com/business/2019/11/11/apple-card-algorithm-sparks-gender-bias-allegations-against-goldman-sachs.

The World Counts. n.d. "Electronic Waste Facts." https://www.theworldcounts.com/stories/electronic-waste-facts.

Torres, É. P. 2022. "Understanding 'Longtermism': Why This Suddenly Influential Philosophy Is So Toxic." Salon, August 20, 2022. https://www.salon.com/2022/08/20/understanding-longtermism-why-this-suddenly-influential-philosophy-is-so.

Vallance, D. 2020. "Forget Brainstorming. Burstiness Is the Key to Creativity." Dropbox Blog, July 22, 2020. https://blog.dropbox.com/topics/work-culture/forget-brainstorming--burstiness-is-the-key-to-creativity--.

Vipra, J. 2024. "Computational Power and AI." AI Now Institute, April 19, 2024. https://ainowinstitute.org/publication/policy/compute-and-ai#h-what-is-compute-and-why-does-it-matter.

Wang, Q., H. Hou, and Z. Li. 2022. "Participative Leadership: A Literature Review and Prospects for Future Research." *Front Psychology, 13,* 924357. https://doi/org/10.3389/fpsyg.2022.924357. PMID: 35719563; PMCID: PMC9204162.

About the Companion Website

This book is accompanied by a companion website:

whatmattersnextbook.com

The website includes:

- A "What Matters Next" action plan template
- Other downloadable resources

Acknowledgments

Thank you to Cheryl, Amanda, Sunnye, Michelle and the whole crew at Wiley for the work it takes to make a book.

Thank you to Annie at Wiley for having recognized an opportunity at Thinkers50.

Thank you to Des Dearlove and Stuart Crainer at Thinkers50 for recognizing my last book and putting me on stage in the first place.

Thank you to all my keynote clients and advisory clients for sharing stories, questions, and what keeps you awake at night so that I could try to help you get some better sleep.

Thank you to all the guests who have joined me for fascinating conversations on *The Tech Humanist Show*. Your input has helped influence my thinking and has shaped the guidance I share with clients and audiences.

Thank you to Mark Levy for caring about this book with me, and tirelessly helping guide this book to its destiny.

Thank you to Ashley Robinson and Erin Daugherty at Interrobang, for such incredible research support for all these years—without whom my research would be a mess.

Thank you to Susan Preiss for being the kind of copywriter another writer can really team up with.

Thank you to Shelley Dolley for helping me imagine I could bring a little Tom Peters magic to my work.

Thank you to Sara Neves whose intrepid brand and web work really gets me. *Muito obrigada.*

Thank you to Lou Diamond and the ThriveLoud Productions team for helping produce *The Tech Humanist Show*.

Thank you to Reed Hastings and Marc Randolph for creating Netflix, which was such a wonderful part of my tech career.

Thank you to Robbie, for always taking the next meaningful step with me, moving forward using all our breath.

About the Author

Kate O'Neill is a digital innovator, chief executive, business writer, and speaker.

Kate is founder and CEO of KO Insights, a strategic advisory firm that improves human experience at scale—especially in data-driven, algorithmically optimized, AI-led interactions.

Her clients and audiences include Adobe, the city of Amsterdam, the city of Austin, Cambridge, Coca-Cola, Colgate-Palmolive, Etsy, Getty Images, Google, Harvard University, IBM, McDonald's, Microsoft, the United Nations, Yale, and Zoom.

Before starting KO Insights, Kate was one of the first 100 employees at Netflix, a technologist at Toshiba, and founder of the groundbreaking analytics firm [meta]marketer.

For her work, Kate has received awards and wide recognition. She was named "Technology Entrepreneur of the Year," a "Power Leader in Technology," a "Woman of Influence," and more, and was featured by Google in the launch of their global campaign for women in entrepreneurship. Thinkers50, a global ranking of top management thinkers, named her to its list of the World's Management Thinkers to Watch and shortlisted her for their Distinguished Award for Digital Thinking.

Her insights have been featured in the *New York Times*, the *Wall Street Journal*, and *WIRED*, and she has appeared as an expert tech commentator on the BBC and NPR.

Known for her ability to make complex topics relatable, Kate is a sought-after keynote speaker, appearing at conferences and corporate events and has spoken to hundreds of thousands of audience members worldwide.

Kate is host and executive producer of the podcast *The Tech Humanist Show*.

She's written six books, including four on business strategy and technology: *Tech Humanist*, *Pixels and Place*, *A Future So Bright*, and *What Matters Next*.

Index

Page numbers followed by *f* refer to figures.

Also by Kate O'Neill

Business Books

A Future So Bright: How Strategic Optimism and Meaningful Innovation Can Restore Our Humanity and Save the World

Tech Humanist: How You Can Make Technology Better for Business and Better for Humans

Pixels and Place: Connecting Human Experience Across Physical and Digital Spaces

Short Reads

Lessons from Los Gatos: How Working at a Startup Called Netflix Made Me a Better Entrepreneur (and Mentor)

Memoir

Surviving Death: What Loss Taught Me About Love, Joy, and Meaning

Contributor to

The Future Starts Now: Expert Insights into the Future of Business, Technology and Society
(Chapter: "Everything is Connected")

Connectedness: How the Best Leaders Create Authentic Human Connection in a Disconnected World
(Chapter: "AI and the Future of Human Connection")

OTHER BOOKS FROM

Thinkers50

Certain Uncertainty
ISBN: 9781394153459

Connectedness
ISBN: 9781394285778

The Upside of Disruption
ISBN: 9781394192601

WILEY